Y0-CDN-432

WORDS OF PRAISE FOR *DESTINY THIEVES*

I loved this book! *Destiny Thieves: Exposing Seducing Spirits* got my attention from beginning to end. Sandie Freed has a unique way of addressing the major "issues and 'Ites'" that we will face in the future if our expected end is to be greater than our beginning. Sandie gives practical steps to break compromise, discouragement and a weakened soulish constitution so we can walk in victory in a changing world. When reading this book, you know that Sandie has learned to submit herself to God and resist the enemies that would stop her from walking in joy and with authority. *Destiny Thieves* is a "treasury of swords" for any prayer warrior who wants to conquer their enemy! As the spiritual war intensifies in days ahead, this is one book that will keep you sharpened and on the offensive in battle!

Chuck D. Pierce
President, Glory of Zion International
Vice President, Global Harvest Ministries

Destiny Thieves does exactly what the title promises – it exposes seducing spirits. Few contemporary writers offer the insight and understanding Sandie Freed shares in her timely and informative work. Using personal experience gained during her years of pastoral ministry and the spiritual perception of an prophetess, she pulls aside the cloak of darkness behind which the enemy has hidden to deceive.

What we do not destroy of the works of the flesh (disobedience, rebellion, etc.), will ultimately rise us to destroy us! The design of the Amalekite spirit is to rob us of our destiny by keeping us unrepentant, disobedient, and deceived. Sandie does a masterful job of explaining how the spirit works and how we can gain victory over its strategies.

The constant words of encouragement offered throughout this manuscript are much appreciated. Though the subject is frightful in its scope, we are made to understand that we have a destiny to fulfill and that our Father, God is committed to us and to our success. The best laid plans of Darkness will not prevent what Jesus intends for His disciples – if we do not remain "ignorant of his (Satan's) devices". *Destiny Thieves* lifts the veil.

Dr. Jim Davis
President, Christian International Apostolic Network

Destiny Thieves is a must read for every church leader and every saint in the Body of Christ. Sandie's insight on the demonic spirits that have been assigned to cut off the individual destinies of people as well as the corporate destiny of the Church is very powerful. These truly are remarkable times for those who are pressing in to fulfill their divine calling. This book will be used as a weapon in the arsenal of believers as they do battle to fulfill their highest call.

Jane Hamon
Apostle and Co-Pastor, Christian International Family Church

Life is full of challenges. Many of them are a result of a spiritual war unseen by the physical eye. To overcome and breakthrough, seeing behind the scene of problems, obstacles and hindrances is essential. Here is a great book, written from practical experience that discusses how to identify the enemy and then what to do about it. Sandie knows what she is talking about it. Read it and you will learn how to overcome and break through.

Barbara J. Yoder
Apostle and Senior Pastor, Shekinah Christian Church
Michigan State Coordinator, United States Strategic Prayer Network
National Apostolic Council, United States Strategic Prayer Network
Breakthrough Apostolic Ministries Network

Destiny Thieves

Exposing Seducing Spirits

Sandie Freed

Destiny Thieves: Exposing Seducing Spirits

Distributed by and Available through:

Sandie Freed

Zion Ministries

P.O. Box 54874

Hurst, TX 76054

Phone: (817) 589-8811

Email: zionministries1@sbcglobal.net

Website: www.ZionMinistries.us

Contents and/or cover may not be copied or reproduced in whole or in part in any form, including any means electronic or recording, without the expressed written consent of the author.

Unless otherwise noted, Scripture quotations in this book are taken from the King James Version of the Bible.

Notes regarding capitalization: "Church" is capitalized when referring to the universal body of believers. When not capitalized, it refers to a local church. "Word" is capitalized when referring to the Holy Bible or Word of God. The name of "satan" is not capitalized unless the name is beginning a sentence.

Copyright © 2005 by Sandie Freed.

All Rights Reserved under International Copyright Law.

Cover design by Tim Cole, Kingdom 3D

ISBN 0-939868-50-4

Second Printing 2005

Printed in the United States of America

For Worldwide Distribution.

Dedication

To my husband, Mickey, who co-labors with me to fulfill destiny and never allows me to "settle" for less than my potential.

To my daughter, Kim Freed Putman, who is still the "best thing I ever did," and her husband, Matt, for their support and love even when I am unlovable.

To my mother, Dena Davis, who is the most courageous and determined woman I know and has always pressed me to be the same.

To my father, Bud Davis, who is fulfilling his eternal destiny in heaven.

Finally, To my Lord, Jesus Christ, who fulfilled His destiny to empower me to fulfill mine.

ACKNOWLEDGEMENTS

Writing a book takes a commitment from an author; however, the author is not alone in fulfilling its completion. There are multitudes involved in this type of project. There are intercessors who pray, families who sacrifice time, and relationships that stand along side supporting the vision. The vision involves attention to a broad-scaled project, but one cannot overlook all of the minute details involved in its completion.

I would like to specifically acknowledge four very precious friends who have stayed awake into the late night hours editing and proofreading. They have also served as my personal intercessors and have prayed me through the completion of this mission. Sarah Amanor, Paula Bledsoe, Vicki Caldwell, and Kathy Shaw, thank you for your support and prayers. I love you guys! We did it!

In addition, I need to thank my sister, Pam Garris and her husband David. This powerful team co-labored with us for so many years and has continued to serve as leaders within Zion Ministries. Pam and David, thank you for continuing to carry the torch!

To all of the ordained and licensed ministers of Zion Ministries, your support has been an underlying strength to me. During times of transition, your faithfulness has been a sustaining force of encouragement.

It is important that I acknowledge Apostles Jim and Jeanni Davis, Apostolic Oversight for Christian International Apostolic Network. I honor and respect you more each year I serve and co-labor with you. You have been examples of faith and perseverance; thank you for your godly example and covenant relationship.

To Apostles Tom and Jane Hamon. Over the years, you were very instrumental in providing needed support and courage as I gained revelation for this book. Thank you for sharing your wisdom and insight concerning spiritual strongholds and discernment. Observing your dedication to the Lord has inspired me to believe for God's very best.

I want to also acknowledge Apostle Leon Walters. You have served on the Board of Zion Ministries for over a decade and labored faithfully with us through the good times as well as the bad times. Mickey and I highly esteem you and thank you for being a mentor as well as a special friend.

To my spiritual parents, Bishop Bill and Mom Evelyn Hamon. Thank you for continuing to believe in me and for challenging me with new opportunities for growth and maturity. I honor you for your determination and commitment to fulfill all that God has for you, and especially for never giving up on me or my destiny.

For all the endless editing and typesetting, I have depended upon Tim Cole. He has remained encouraging as well as patient with all the rushed, last minute re-types. Thank you!

And, I want to thank the staff, members and leaders of Faith Christian Center, who served the Lord with us during the years that we pastored (1990-2004).This book involves fourteen years of research and study. Your support through the years made it possible for me to find strength as I pressed for revelation needed for this book. We worshiped together, co-labored together and fulfilled destiny together. God bless each of you as you continue moving forward into your divine fulfillment.

CONTENTS

Foreword

We who believe that God created mankind for a divine purpose believe Adam and Eve were created with a destiny to fulfill. Before Adam and Eve were created there was one of God's angelic beings who rebelled against God, was cast out of heaven and became an opposer of all that God destines to happen. This being became known as Satan, the devil, prince of darkness, etc. Satan seduced 1/3 of the angels into joining him. When they were cast out of heaven to earth they became evil seducing spirits. Adam and Eve were seduced by Satan causing them to fail to fulfill their destiny of filling the earth with mankind creation in God's own image and likeness. Jesus came and provided redemption for mankind to become a new creation with the destiny to be in God's image and likeness. Those who have accepted Jesus Christ as Savior and Lord have a divine destiny to fulfill. Satan has a host of "Destiny Thieves" who have been commissioned by Satan to stop God's people from fulfilling their membership ministry in the Body of Christ and divine destiny on Earth.

Sandie Freed has unveiled the manipulative deceitful and seductive tactics used by Satan to prevent, hinder and stop God's people from fulfilling their destiny. This book will be a liberating force to set captives free and equip the saints with revelation knowledge and spiritual truth that will enable them to avoid the traps of the enemy and to overcome when tempted. Knowing truth enables one to fulfill destiny.

The truths and divine insights revealed in this book need to be known by every saint and especially those who are in leadership positions. As each chapter is read you will think, "this is great, helpful and so enlightening." When you begin to think that there couldn't be much more truth on this matter then read on. For the next chapter is even more enlightening and enabling.

One of the hidden blessings is the realization that everyone's calling and destiny is as diverse as are the different members of the human body. Some are called to build great works for God such as mega churches and world-wide organizations. Others are called to go through certain processes, experiences and ministries that cause them to discover great truths that bless mankind. This is what Sandie is doing by writing this book. In the natural and according to mankind's standards Jesus didn't accomplish much. Nevertheless Christ fulfilled His destiny even though Satan tried to steal His destiny by tempting Jesus with success according to man's standards.

Sandie and Micky Freed have experienced many things that has resulted in revelation knowledge that will enable millions of Christians to fulfill their destiny. Sandie did not receive these divine insights by just reading books. She received them from being on the front line of ministry, personal experience in dealing with people and supernaturally discovering the "Destiny Thieves" that are sent from hell to stop Christians from fulfilling their calling in Christ Jesus.

Thanks Sandie for allowing God to take you through the challenging processes to bring forth these vital truths to the people of God everywhere. This book is destined to be a vital tool for enabling Christian to fulfill their calling and destiny.

Dr. Bill Hamon

Chairman, Founder and Bishop of Christian International Ministries Network
Founder of Christian International Apostolic Network
Author of Seven Major Books:

> The Eternal Church
> Prophets and Personal Prophecy
> Prophets and The Prophetic Movement
> Prophets, Pitfalls and Principles
> Apostles, Prophets and The Coming Moves of God
> The Day of the Saints
> Who Am I and Why Am I Here

I Want To Live and Fulfill Destiny!

Destiny: something to which a person or thing is destined; a predetermined course of events[1].

O*h, Lord, please let this be a good report!* It was such a desperate plea that I began to beg. *Please, Lord, I have stood on Your Word, I have done all I know to do, I do not want to die!* These words silently repeated themselves as I dialed my physician's office for the latest results of my blood tests.

Anyone who has been forced to wait for laboratory reports has identified with the tormenting fear that occurred during the delays. It is especially more severe when you are sensing the spirit of death lurking at the door just waiting for the opportunity to seize your hope and life.

The secretary placed me on hold. More anxiety flooded my thoughts. With my heart beating more rapidly, a cold sweat was forming upon my brow, and suddenly my legs felt as if they were literally buckling beneath me.

I prepared myself as I waited for the nurse to return to the phone.

If I receive another bad report, how will I respond this time?

I had, up to this point, found the strength to move forward. Somehow, I had been empowered to dig down deep within my spirit and found enough faith to have risen up and believed that God WOULD come through for me.

Would it be different this time? I felt that I had come to the end of my rope!

*God, I absolutely **cannot** find renewed strength to go on!*

I soon found myself running to the bedroom, sobbing. I threw myself across the bed. Another blood test and negative report had shaken me to the core. The latest "death sentence" poisoned my thoughts and emotions...I had little hope left, I concluded.

"Will this battle against this destructive viral infection EVER end?" I screamed aloud while pleading for my life.

"I can't take this any more, God! I just can't take it! I am going to die and I have not fulfilled my destiny!"

I have now realized that I did not fully understand the meaning of **destiny**. All I understood at the time was that I felt extremely void and desperate for life. I wanted to do so much for the Lord, but did not understand how it could ever manifest. I now understand that everyone endures a **process of preparation** while fulfilling destiny and that God has desired results for each of us that complete His planned destiny.

For me, it was a long battle continuing to choose life. At the time, I did not possess the revelation that what I was experiencing was part of the **process** in "the making of a minister." Every mountain of tribulation, every test, every wilderness experience was the needed preparation for the **possessing of my Promised Land.** While enduring each storm, it became increasingly difficult finding the light through the dark clouds. Through every tunnel of darkness I traveled, I was forced to trust the Lord and find strength in His ability to sustain and guide me.

Hindsight is 20/20 vision and, looking back, I fully understand that the Lord desired to become my compass. It was as if I were a ship captain being trained to follow a spiritual compass while I sailed through rough seas during stormy conditions. The training I was receiving was to not focus on the storm, but rather focus on His Word and His report in every situation. I was involved in boot-camp training exercising levels of greater faith. This was all necessary for a future destiny that He had planned for my life.

During this particular storm, it felt like a hurricane! The winds were so fierce my ship was being tossed back and forth. I felt as if I were thrown to the edge and about to be tossed overboard! I didn't know if I could persevere because there seemed to be no strength left to fight. I felt as if I could not hold on any longer.

In the natural it appeared that death was imminent. There seemed to be nothing I could do about this situation and I found myself totally out of control. My situation seemed hopeless. "There is nothing else I can do now except lie down and die," I continued to cry out begging God to help me.

"Lord," I said His name in between sobs, "If You will let me live, I promise to serve You. If You will extend my life, I will serve You with every fiber of my being…for the rest of my entire life I will do whatever You want me to do!"

Have you ever felt that there were mountains in your life that seemed insurmountable? Are you crying out to possess your determined end? If so, then read on! In the following chapters you will gain understanding of the Destiny Thieves that rob your future along with strategies to empower your faith and achieve victory and destiny.

If only I had understood and possessed the determination and faith of Caleb, the Old Testament example of courage and vision to possess his mountain! The scripture states that Caleb had another spirit. This meant that Caleb was *different* than the rest of the twelve spies who surveyed Canaan. A further Word study reveals that Caleb was *different* in the fact that he *followed* God to the fullest. The plans that God had for Caleb's possession were *predetermined* and were a part of Caleb's *destiny*! There was a planned destiny of possession for Caleb and for Caleb's generations. But also there would be warfare; Caleb would have to FIGHT for the possession of his mountain. His destiny involved defeating the Canaanites and the Amalekites; the two strongholds that you and I also must overcome to receive our inheritance! In order to fully inherit my destiny, I needed to change my thinking, rise up with great courage, move forward and defeat the "ites" of Canaan; especially the Amalekite stronghold that blocked my destiny.

But My servant Caleb, because he has a different spirit in him and has followed Me fully, I will bring into the land where he went, and his descendants shall inherit it.

Now the Amalekites and the Canaanites dwell in the valley; tomorrow turn and move out into the wilderness by the Way of the Red Sea.

Numbers 14:24-25

Yet, at this time Caleb and his victory were not anywhere on my radar screen! Another few minutes of sobbing followed. Again, more pleas for life continued, "Lord, I have not yet begun to fulfill my destiny. I haven't done enough to serve you. Please let me fulfill your plans for my life."

Suddenly, I felt impressed to read Jeremiah 29:11 which read:

"For I know the thoughts that I think toward you, saith the LORD, thoughts of peace, and not of evil, to give you an expected end."

I meditated on this passage. "What is an expected end?" I mumbled as I curiously sought out the <u>Strong's Concordance</u> or any handy Word study. Was the Lord actually telling me that He would heal me? Did He REALLY have a destiny for me to fulfill? Did He have plans for me that I was not aware of?

I later realized that the answer to all of my questions was YES!

God DID have a plan for my life. God DID plan for me to fulfill destiny, He had an "expected end" of fulfillment for me.

The "Expected End"

The phrase **expected end** actually means *an <u>expectation</u> and <u>ground</u> of hope. It also implies that we are to lie in wait for (hope) and also translates to bind together (as if we are to bind our hope and expectations together to achieve an expected end!)²*

How exciting to realize that God desired to give me **ground** to hope…a foundation of hope upon which I needed to build with words of faith. With later revelation of this passage I realized that the Lord was giving me a "rhema"

Word. This word from God was the fertile soil into which He had provided for me to sow. As I would continue to plant His promises into that soil of divine hope, then I would surely achieve my destiny. From that point, I was able to bind every promise together giving me great expectations for my miracle. For the first time since I developed the viral infection, I was able to BELIEVE! I had expectation and hope firmly stabilized within my spirit. Now, every promise God gave me was sown into the ground of hope and expectation.

But, the miracle did not come suddenly; I labored for my healing. Many fears and mindsets had become roadblocks to breakthrough. The barriers of uncertainties were similar to computer chips of negativity, which were deeply imbedded in my mind; the grim outlook seemed impossible to dislodge. However, the process of coming out of my wilderness of death and infirmity was perfecting me for a later calling.

At this time of my life I did not understand how much God loved me. I was convinced that I was destined to die prematurely; after all…the doctors said I would die. I had been pressing into God for months, believing by faith I was to be healed. Being tormented during the night seasons with disturbing dreams concerning death, I was bombarded with discouragement, confusion and exhaustion. My faith eventually gave way to the spirit of death and each day seemed to be filled with tormenting thoughts of funeral services.

Then finally, a phone call came that changed my life.

"Sandie, you have got to go with me to Christian International and let the prophets minister life to you!" It was my friend on the phone. She had been praying for my recovery for months on end.

"Go where? What is Christian International?"

"Well," she began to inform me, "It is an organization founded by Dr. Bill Hamon. He has gathered a company of prophets that know how to hear from God. I believe you need to go and ask the prophets to minister life to you. I just know they are a key to releasing your destiny!"

My exposure to the prophetic ministry was limited, but I did understand the power of the prophetic word. Years earlier a prophet had ministered a personal word to me. The prophetic word and insight was so accurate and the anointing so tangible there was no doubt that God was in the midst.

Could this be the time of my breakthrough? Could this be my opportunity to be released into destiny? "When can we go?" I jumped at the chance for life!

Within a few weeks we were on an airplane headed for Florida to attend a Christian International Prophetic Conference, a conference that radically changed my life. It was there that I received an impartation for transformation and a release into fulfilling destiny.   Prophets Dr. Mary Crum and Dr. Leon Walters (both ordained ministers with Christian International) ministered that God had a destiny for me to fulfill, that God was NOT finished with me yet! Their words, "You shall live and not die and proclaim the word of the Lord," still resound through my spirit as I remember the first time they ministered to me.

When I received these words, I leaped from my chair and began to shout for joy! Suddenly, the revelation of Jeremiah 29:11 became reality and a revelation. It was at that time I realized that God DID have a plan for me and that He had healing and restoration planned for my life. God had "good thoughts" and not "evil thoughts" toward me and He had expectations for me to fulfill. He had an **expected end**!

It was only a few days later that I heard Bishop Bill Hamon, who later became my spiritual father, minister on the spirit of Caleb. Caleb overcame the wilderness, doubt and unbelief and gained possession of his promised mountain. Caleb's positive report "Give Me My Mountain!" began to take root in my heart..."Lord, I have a destiny and I will fulfill it!" Finally, hope had been planted **firmly** in my ground...I now believed, beyond any doubt, that my destiny could be fulfilled.

Becoming Determined for Destiny

This was my NEW beginning. My life was totally transformed due to the prophetic insight I received. I had a destiny and I became DETERMINED for DESTINY. I knew in my heart that it was time to set my face like flint toward my future and desired end.

By being determined, we are being "staunch and unwavering." It also means that we are to decide; implying that we must make a decision and then not waver in that decision.[3] In order for me to move forward in conquest, I had to finally decide that I wanted whatever God had for my future and then lock into hope and faith, not wavering.

Possession is a three-step process. First, we must make a firm decision to move forward. Second, we are to set our faces like flint toward destiny. And the third step is to walk in the empowerment of His grace to move forward and possess our mountain of inheritance.

It was a two-year battle with the spirit of death before I was completely healed from the viral infection. For two years my husband and I warred with my prophetic word before I experienced the faithfulness of His promise. We were faithful as Paul instructed Timothy "… to wage the good warfare…" over my prophecies for breakthrough (see 1 Timothy 1:18). Many hours were spent playing our taped prophetic words, pacing the floor together and declaring God's Word over my body. There DID come the time that I heard the doctors say these glorious words…

Sandie, there are no test results reporting any more infection!

Yes, finally, I was beginning to fulfill destiny, the beginning of the plans and expected end of which God speaks. My mountain of death dissolved, just as the Lord had promised. I am now an ordained prophetess of the Lord receiving the spiritual oversight of Dr. Bill Hamon. My husband and I pastored Faith Christian Center in Bedford, Texas for fourteen years and now have established Zion Ministries Apostolic/ Prophetic Training Center in the same area. We travel extensively representing Christian International Apostolic Network. Together as an apostolic-prophetic team we are fulfilling the Ephesians 4:11 commission of the five-fold ministry; training and equipping the saints to do the work of the ministry.

When I look over my shoulder into the past and observe how far the grace of God has brought me I am often overwhelmed. I would have never dreamed that God had so many wonderful plans for my life. To ever consider that He could desire to use me to train others in the prophetic ministry, dreams and visions, counseling, intercession, miracles and other spiritual giftings is amazing to me! I felt as if I were a NOTHING going NOWHERE! I saw myself as sick, weak, mentally incapable yet God saw me as healed, strong and being used for His kingdom. Wow! I HAVE BEEN GOING SOMEWHERE (IN HIM) EVER SINCE I GRABBED HOLD OF DESTINY!

YOU Have a Destiny

Did you know that YOU also have a destiny? That YOU also have an "expected end" that God has planned? That YOU can also possess the courage, strength and determination of Caleb to possess your mountain? Maybe you are in a situation similar to mine. Maybe you have experienced hopeless situations and you feel as if you are not fulfilling your potential. Maybe you are desperate for answers to your situations.

You may not have experienced the life-altering change I encountered through the prophetic ministry of a prophet, but please understand this....the Bible is full of prophetic words! Yes, the Bible speaks the Word of God and His desires of good things for your life. His plans for you are just as they are for me....good and not evil! All through the Word of God are prophecies of life, healing, restoration, and fulfillment.

There Is An Enemy!

But also realize this...there is an enemy, the Prince of this world who has a plan of destruction. The devil, our adversary, comes to steal, kill and destroy (see John 10:10). He is a thief and he desires to steal your destiny. He has many different tactics to snatch you out from the plans of God. There are quite possibly strongholds in your land of promise. The Amalekites, a tribe who robs destiny, are probably in your territory and must be driven out in order to possess your promise.

Each of us is an Esther, having the favor of the Lord and born for such a time as this. But she also had an enemy, Haman the Agagite, (a descendent of the Amalekites) who plotted to destroy her, her family, and her entire race! The devil does not simply desire to destroy you; he wants your entire family, business, church and nation! And he will not stop there...I have said many times that if you ask the devil to dinner, he will bring his entire suitcase. He has plans to REMAIN if we open any door and allow entrance.

If you have ever vowed to serve God, the devil will come to steal your confession. I vowed that if He would heal me, I would be obedient to serve him and do WHATEVER He asked. My vows were tested many times but God gave me the grace to achieve victory.

Throughout the years the Lord has revealed many different strongholds that destroy the seeds of destiny. **This book reveals the different satanic strategies that rob God's children of potential, but also many divine strategies for victory that will prove helpful in your journey toward total fulfillment.**

We are at war. We are God's army. Yes, this will be a battle, but a battle very worthwhile! Remember this one thing....There is no great victory without a battle!

Onward, Christian Soldiers!

Prayer

Father, you are in control of our destiny. You are the Alpha and the Omega, the Beginning and the End. Your Word says that You have plans for each of us and You have good thoughts towards us. Lord, we thank You for every good thought and every good plan that You have ordained for us. You are the Author and Finisher of our faith. Thank You for imparting a new measure of faith within us. We choose life and we choose to believe that You have a destiny for each of us to fulfill. Thank You for empowering us to fulfill Your plans in us and for us. This day we choose to set our faces like flint. We choose to be obedient vessels, observing Your Word and being faithful to walk in the direction You have chosen for us. We choose to be like Caleb, ones of a different spirit to fully follow after Your future plans for us. We are determined to serve You. We declare that our household will continue to serve You all the days of our lives! Now, Lord, open our hearts and minds to new revelation so that we may fully embrace whatever steps are needed to fulfill our destiny and TAKE OUR MOUNTAIN!

Amen.

Important Definitions to Consider

Thief: someone who <u>steals,</u> especially <u>secretly</u>[4]

Steal: to take without permission or right, especially <u>secretly</u> or by force[5].

Secret: something <u>hidden</u> from sight, without general knowledge.[6]

Exposure: an act of revealing or unmasking[7]

Seduction: the act of being seduced, led astray from duty or principles; corrupt, attract, win over and entice.[8]

It is time to <u>unmask</u> and <u>expose</u> the <u>secret</u> strategies of <u>seduction</u> by the Destiny Thieves!

Chapter One

DESTINY THIEVES

The thief cometh not, but for to steal, and to kill, and to destroy: I am come that they might have life, and that they might have it more abundantly.

John 10:10

It was a Sunday morning. My expectations were rising up within my spirit, believing God for a divine visitation. It was a lovely spring day; the sun was beaming, just short of a glare, through the windshield as I drove to church. It seemed as if I could almost reach out and touch God's glory, I was so full of faith! I turned up the volume of my favorite cassette and tried desperately to outsing the singers on the tape, "jiving and nodding" as I lifted my voice to the Lord.

Nothing can steal my joy today! I thought to myself. *This is the day the Lord has made and I will rejoice and be glad in it!*

My fingers tapped against the steering wheel, keeping beat with the drum sounds echoing through the speakers. I felt like a teenager moving my entire body along with the music. Why I could even rap to this! I was totally boasting in my good day.

I wheeled into the parking lot of our church where we had been pastoring for over a decade. The crepe myrtles were blooming in fragrance; the flowerbeds were birthing the fruits of planted seeds.

The grounds are well manicured and beautiful; it's a wonderful day!

I acknowledged a familiar face and waved as I found my designated parking place. I glanced at another vehicle entering the parking lot and waved again, still smiling and joyful.

I made my way into the building, humming to the music that was still playing in my head. As I advanced toward the office I was met by one of our members who served on our pastoral team. I greeted him with a smile, yet noticed the unreturned gesture. From his expression, it did not take a rocket scientist to discern that something would attempt to destroy my good day.

My heart sank. *Not more bad news! I silently groaned as my emotions ran amuck. Oh, Lord, this is too beautiful a day to have it spoiled. When will this ever end?*

I sat down to prepare myself for another negative report concerning our congregation. I thought the battle was over and that we were experiencing breakthrough; the devil, however, was still at work.

The Accuser of the Brethren

And I heard a loud voice saying in heaven, Now is come salvation, and strength, and the kingdom of our God, and the power of his Christ: for the <u>accuser of our brethren</u> is cast down, which accused them before our God day and night.

Rev 12:10 (emphasis mine)

Six months earlier we were tempted to resign as pastors, to basically throw in the towel. Actually, not just one towel…but rather EVERY towel we had ever owned and used in any capacity! Now, after standing for such a lengthy season and finally experiencing a breakthrough, we were finding ourselves back into battle against more of the enemy's plans of destruction.

My husband and I had been senior pastors for years. Our ability to survive and remain in the Christian race consisted of continual re-commitments and re-newed decisions to "lock back in" to fulfill destiny. The battle with the accuser of the brethren had been relentless. It seemed as if we could barely catch our breath from a previous onslaught before another "air raid" targeted us. At times I even imagined myself enlisted in the Air Force during World War II, flying a dive-bomber while dodging bullets from the enemy.

Leaving Our Post

The care pastor followed me to my office and I prepared my heart, my emotions, and my mind to hear the results of another evil assignment. Once again I bowed my head as I was informed that one of our leaders had forsaken the "call" and had chosen to leave the ministry and backslide into an old life-style. His wife and he had returned to their spiritual Egypt, deciding it was too difficult to live for the Lord. The leader had left his post, forsaken his anointing and retreated into a "comfortable" place. My heart sank in despair.

He was so gifted, I silently told the Lord, we needed him…we had so many plans to _use him_ in ministry. I was sad that we lost him because he was special to us. We had known him for years, mentored him and observed his spiritual growth toward maturity. And I became even more discouraged to lose another quality leader to "comfort zones." Actually I was being somewhat selfish; my husband and I desperately needed dedicated and proven servants and here we were, losing one of proven quality.

After the conversation, I closed my office door. Immediately tears filled my eyes and found their way down my face. Once again, I began crying out loud, begging God for an answer.

"Why, God, why? What is happening to our leaders? They are constantly being attacked and they quit. Just when they are on the verge of breakthrough, they give up!" I poured out my concerns to the Lord.

The Thief

The Lord answered with an astounding vision. I saw a strong seducing spirit, in the form of a thief. This thief was successfully stealing God's leaders, seductively drawing them away from their position and inheritance.

First, he would seduce them into believing the lie that they didn't belong, that they didn't "fit" any longer. As a result, each of them would separate from the Church body. Once he had them alone, unprotected and vulnerable, he would strip them of their power and authority; stealing their destiny. Before the enemy convinced them to exit, we would notice complaints such as:

"I can't find my place in the body."

"I don't seem to have a place anymore."

"No one cares about me in this church,"

"No one calls me any more. I need a church that cares."

Even though we made many attempts to contact the sheep and tried every possible way to prove our love and concern, it was never enough. They had already been separated in their hearts.

Jezebel

The seducing spirit in the vision was in the form of a type of Jezebel; the "painted lady" in the scriptures who dressed seductively, murdered the prophets and threatened to destroy Elijah (see 1 Kings 18,19, 2 Kings 9:30). In the vision her countenance changed from a seductive-type person into a thief or bandit-type character. Once more, a third time, the countenance transformed into a person plagued with uncleanness and defilement. The spirit had no gender.

I knew in my spirit that the thief represented Jezebel, the idolatrous queen who stole Naboth's inheritance. She worked in unity with the sons of Belial, falsely accusing Naboth, stealing and then murdering him (1 Kings 31). The vision revealed that the seducing spirit was also a perverted, unclean spirit (the Jezebel and the unclean spirit are further explained in Chapters 11 and 12).

Our church was not experiencing an isolated attack; this was the enemy's strategy against every ministry, which made an impact in the Spirit-realm! In the vision it was clear that the result of this demonically inspired attack was the seduction and apostasy of godly leaders and saints. The spirit of deception was so over-powering that it was deceiving the elect!

Then, I heard the Lord speak concerning the sheep and the precious servants that He had appointed to support us. The vision continued to unfold and the

Lord revealed that there was an assignment planned to steal the anointing and destiny from His chosen ones. Saints who had tremendous calls of God upon their lives were being attacked and seduced. The enemy had convinced them that it was just "too hard" to remain in the race, so they got out! I knew, once again, this was not for just our own church but for the Church at large.

The vision further revealed a clear strategy of satan. If he could seduce the supporters of ministry (the Aarons and Hurs and potential leaders) then we have no one to hold up our arms. As a result we, as Senior Pastors, would become weary and unable to continue to go forth. The plans of our enemy became obvious; the thief would steal our leaders and servants, thus stealing <u>our</u> strength and support. With very few around to support us, we could not continue to be effective in ministry. Since we are all called to be leaders and servants in the Kingdom, this vision affects the entire Body of Christ.

The Devil's J-O-B

Did you ever wonder what the devil's REAL job is? I mean like his J-O-B, you know, like the job where you punch a time clock and get paid to work? Yes, the 9-5 routine. Only the devil is at work 24-7!

In times past, when I would pray to strategize and develop counter-attacks, I thought he just showed up periodically with his "hit" list, and then would retreat for a while until it was time to smack me again. Similar to the mafia, I believed that satan would have his network of syndicated crime and when the evil godfather released his periodic hit lists, all hell would break loose!

We observe in Scripture that his day <u>and</u> night job is to wear us out!

> *And he shall speak great words against the most High, and shall <u>wear out</u> the saints of the most High, and think to change times and laws: and they shall be given into his hand until a time and times and the dividing of time.*

> Daniel 7:25 (emphasis mine)

What does that actually indicate? It means our enemy will attempt to do whatever it takes to obtain such a hold on us that we will quit running the race and abort the fulfillment of destiny. He is compulsively focused and determined to exhaust us with long, weary battles, extensive spiritual warfare, and seducing lies that threaten our relationship with God. All this is done to weaken our spiritual and physical strength and faith. He is diligent with his work schedule (it being BOTH day and night), and he is completely dedicated to his cause. He even works during his lunch break, walking before God falsely accusing the saints of God. Friends, this guy never takes a vacation; he is dedicated to wearing us out! This is why it is extremely important that we must understand his determination and rise up in spiritual warfare against him.

Know this one thing before we go further...we have already won the battle! The blood of Jesus has cleansed us and strengthened us to go forth into great victory. But in order to win, we must understand his tactics and the strategies of the **destiny thief.** Every good soldier studies the maneuvers of his enemy in order to cut him off at the pass!

Jezebel and the Accuser Steal Destiny!

The accuser of the brethren is continually working with demonic governmental structures of evil authority to discredit the saints and undermine spiritual authority. The demonic assignments attempt to falsely accuse leaders and servants while at the same time stripping away their confidence. The Body of Christ becomes convinced that they are ineffective and that God is unable to vindicate them from the vicious lies and rumors.

Once the sheep are wounded and inactive, an even greater bomb explodes; Jezebel hits her target! A Jezebel stronghold moves into the congregation to control the atmosphere   through worship and intercession and prophetic ministry. Her main target is now pointed against the leaders as she attempts every known strategy to discredit them with false accusations and undermine their authority. Preying upon the sheep, she seeks out the weak first...spreading lies and division. Only a short time will pass before there is a church split, or the leadership is torn apart, intercession is halted, and worship is stifled...all because a demon is simply doing his JOB!

As most pastors can testify, this spirit attempts to stir up a congregation with strife, competition, false accusations and false prophecy.

The Book of Revelations reveals that the ACCUSER will falsely testify against the saints of God (see Rev 12:10). The accuser's purpose is to promote disunity, which will steal the life of any ministry. Looking closely at the enemy's strategy is to understand that since unity releases life, then disunity will release death. Ps. 133 states that unity flows from the headship down and that there is a release of greater anointing when the congregation is in unity. Since the anointing breaks off yokes of oppression, it stands to reason why the enemy plots to destroy the anointing. If there is not unity then there is no anointing flowing to the Body of Christ!

> *And it shall come to pass in that day, that his burden shall be taken*
> *away from off thy shoulder, and his yoke from off thy neck, and the*
> *yoke shall be destroyed because of the anointing.*

Isaiah 10:27

The only way to overcome this spirit is by proclaiming the blood of Jesus and the victory of the blood, using our testimony against him and also loving not our own lives unto death.

> *10) And I heard a loud voice saying in heaven, Now is come salvation, and strength, and the kingdom of our God, and the power of his Christ: for the accuser of our brethren is cast down, which accused them before our God day and night.*
> *11) And they overcame him by the blood of the Lamb, and by the word of their testimony; and they loved not their lives unto the death.*

Revelation 12:10-11 (emphasis mine)

Victory in Blood

Each time we have battled the accuser of the brethren we have laid down our lives once more and committed to the "higher calling" with a more determined effort. Since the devil has desired to steal our destiny, the accuser has hit hard and strategically targeted every ministry that is dedicated to training the saints. Ministries with the mandate to fulfill Ephesians 4:11, dedicated to training and equipping the saints, will be facing an evil assignment of destruction.

We have also realized that we must spiritually draw a "blood line" and declare that the enemy cannot step through the boundary of the blood of Jesus. We had to constantly declare the power of the blood of Jesus and remind the devil that we have the victory because of the blood. Many times I have visited the sick in the hospitals and taken red ribbon. I deliberately cut the ribbon and would tie it to their hospital beds as a sign of the bloodline being drawn in the spirit realm. This is an example of a prophetic act, which demonstrated a spiritual principle to the devil. We would join together in prayer, plead the blood of Jesus Christ, draw the bloodline and command satan and the spirits of death to leave the premises. As a result, God's power and anointing would come and stay the hand of premature death.

Victory in Testimony

Another area of victory is through our testimonies. We must continually remind the devil of what the Lord has done for us and to testify of His goodness and His promises. In the middle of battle it is often difficult to focus on God's goodness, however when we press through to proclaim God's power and His Word, it breaks the assignment against us! We must understand that when the accuser comes, he wants to cause our minds to be confused and affect us to the degree that we feel we cannot testify about God's love and faithfulness. If we succumb to his pressure and believe his lies, and then we cannot battle the accuser at all. At that very time of crisis is when we need to be more determined to give our testimony. We must rise up and begin to declare the works of the Lord and our testimony of His goodness will insure the defeat of the accuser!

The Many faces of Seduction

During the vision about the destiny thief, (see Chapter 1) and its planned seduction, I pressed in even further for more revelation. The Lord spoke very clearly that He was taking me on a journey to understand how the seducing spirit works through the **Accuser of the Brethren**, the **Amalekite** stronghold, the spirits of **Jezebel** and **Belial** along with the **unclean and religious spirits** (all spirits are discussed later). He promised to release keys of understanding that would open up doors of victory, if only I would remain obedient to my own destiny to serve Him. This journey to understand the strategies of the enemy has taken several years and revelation continues to unfold. One sure thing I have realized is that we must continually be **determined for destiny** and maintain the spirit of Caleb or the seducing spirits will ensnare us at every turn! I have desired to quit the ministry more times than I care to mention. However, God was faithful to bring breakthrough after breakthrough and I have remained determined to fulfill my destiny and take my mountain!

As I have pressed in for further revelation, I have become more and more encouraged. I have a renewed faith in His divine ability to deliver me from ALL oppression of my enemy and that there is nothing too difficult for God (see Jer.32: 17). He and I make a majority and as long as I am obedient. Then, all areas work together for my good (see Romans 8:28). Our church survived another crisis and we grew to new levels of faith and revelation. And, oh yes, we gained understanding of the Destiny Thieves which is the reason for this book. Read on!

Chapter Two

Overcoming the "Perilous Times"

This know also, that in the last days <u>perilous times</u> shall come.

2 Timothy 3:1 (emphasis mine)

Quick! Turn on the television in the bedroom! An airplane has crashed into the World Trade Center!"

My husband, Mickey, jolted from the bed.

"What?" Half asleep he grabbed his slippers and housecoat and made his way to the television.

The devastation of **911** (September 11, 2001) was televised on every possible channel and aired worldwide. Hearts across the nation sank with the newly discovered threats of terrorism.

For days the media committed to "round the clock" testimonies while the world anxiously waited for updated reports. Millions camped in front of televisions, totally fear stricken, as terrorist assignments were unmasked. Many people even feared it to be "the end of the world."

The tragedy <u>stole</u> the lives of loved ones and millions of people grieved along with the families of the deceased.

The **911 tragedy** was not limited to America; it was a calamity which affected the entire world. In fact, it literally "turned our world upside down!" Fear wreaked havoc as millions of people panicked. It seemed as if the world actually stood still when airline travel and other methods of transportation were cut to minimums. Economic systems began to suffer and became even more crippling as the stock market took a downward spiral.

Terrorist threats manifested in new methods, now we were aware of chemical warfare in a different dimension. Anthrax became a new word in our vocabulary. Suddenly, our total environment along with anything that is needed for LIFE was threatened. Our lakes and rivers needed for drinking water, fields of grain, orchards of fruit, farmlands of vegetables and even livestock were all possibly defiled through terrorist strategies to destroy us.

Troubled Times

We live in very "*perilous*" times and the enemy thrives in fearful situations. In fact, he will even devise plans against us to create fear!

The word perilous is a Greek word translating as "troubled." The *Enhanced Strong's Lexicon* goes further to translate the word as being dangerous to the point of being *fierce* and *savage*. It also states that the word relates to becoming slackened and relaxed and going from a <u>higher place to a lower place</u>.[9]

When we carefully examine 2 Timothy 3:1, we begin to gain revelation concerning the end times. Through word studies, it is clear that in the end times the enemy and his cohorts will release a savage onslaught that will be extremely **fierce**. I am sure that you will agree with me that **911** was a **fierce** attack! But I believe it was much more than a terrorist assignment, it is also a demonic strategy of destruction!

We live in troubled times when seducing spirits are extremely active. Their plan is to strip us of all faith in God's ability to provide for us and cause us to focus on fear and tragedy.

I am confident that much of the enemy's **fierce** attack is targeted against the saints of the Most High. The assignment has been planned to be so very fierce that it would seduce others to leave the faith or become lukewarm in their love for God. The enemy has strategies that seduce God's children into compromise resulting in moving from <u>higher places</u> of authority to <u>lower positions.</u>

Is it any wonder that believers are consistently under attack? The devil wants to steal your destiny and authority! How many times have you known you have had a destiny of authority in God's kingdom only to find yourself desiring to quit the race and run in the opposite direction?

Fulfilling the High Calling

Many of God's children are quitting the race! During these fierce and troubled times pastors and other ministers have left their positions. Saints are compromising morality and integrity for fame and fortune. Some are settling for a lower call, a lower position, and later choosing a different route than what God has destined for each of them which is the "high calling" of Christ.

Philippians 3:14 states that "we are to press toward the mark for the prize of the high calling…" and yet the enemy has pressured multitudes into settling for lower positions and defeated destiny.

To make this even clearer, allow me to show you step by step what happens during the seasons of "perilous times" as the enemy would attempt to attack us:

1) it is a **dangerous** time
2) it is so dangerous that the attacks from the enemy can be **fierce** and even **savage**
3) **seducing spirits** are extremely active
4) the enemy strategizes to seduce us into becoming **slack** and **relaxed** in our commitments to God
5) if we do slack off or get relaxed we are **removed from a higher place** (in authority) **to a lower place** (in authority)

And here are some steps to overcome the perilous times (and attacks!)

1) **pray!**

2) put on the **full armor** of God and take a firm combat position in spiritual warfare

3) activate your gift of **spiritual discernment**

4) use the **keys of the kingdom**, binding all power of the enemy and loosing the perfect will of God

5) be on guard and **spiritually alert** at all times

6) become more **committed** to serve God

7) **do not compromise**!

8) **remain accountable** to authority

Satan, the False Prophet
During perilous times, a spirit of false prophesy will arise!

What do you think of when you imagine a false prophet? Do you envision a wild man who speaks as a loose cannon spouting weird words and prophecies, which make no sense at all? Do you believe a false prophet is limited to someone who "misses it" while delivering a prophetic word? Well, dear ones, I have realized that *satan* will falsely prophesy to you; especially during perilous and troubled seasons of your life! He will speak to your mind and seduce you to believe a lie and make unwise choices. He will lead you in wrong directions and then persuade you to "go his way" rather than to "go God's way." The enemy's voice may even sound like God's voice.

What?! I can almost hear some of you questioning that statement. You are most likely wondering how God and the devil could possibly sound alike. Well, actually they don't. The problem is that too many of us don't talk and listen to God enough to quickly discern the correct voice.

Don't Be Deceived!

Satan's voice is very seductive and many times his voice is more familiar because we spend too much time listening to him! The Scripture states that satan is transformed as an angel of light (see 2 Cor. 11:14). Light is scripturally symbolic of truth. Therefore, according to God's Word, satan's words will sometimes <u>sound</u> like truth. If we are not properly trained to hear and discern the Father's voice, we can be deceived. Each of us must become committed to spiritual training so that we quickly recognize His voice. Through proper use of discernment we will not easily be seduced by the enemy to believe lies.[10] Spending more intimate time with the Father guarantees levels of accuracy in discerning the true Light.

Many of God's children do not believe they can be deceived. I have been amazed at the number of Christians who fall prey to an angel of light. Even mature believers are vulnerable to this seducing spirit. In fact, we must ALL remain on guard; remember the scripture states that false prophets will come and if possible deceive the very elect!

> *For there shall arise false Christs, and false prophets, and shall shew great signs and wonders; insomuch that, if it were possible, they shall **deceive the very elect***

> Matthew 24:24 (my emphasis)

There are many avenues of satan's deception. Don't look for him to come as he did in the past because he often chooses different doors. The devil lies in wait for the right time to attack you. He will seek any available entrance to abort destiny. According to Matthew 26:41 we must continue to watch and pray so that we do not enter into temptation.

> *Watch and pray, that ye enter not into temptation: the spirit indeed is willing, but the flesh is weak.*

Church Prayer and Intercession

Perilous times will provoke us to prayer. In fact, we will not survive the seduction of satan if we are not watchful and in prayer. However, be aware that the devil hates prayer and because it is so powerful, he will strategize to dismantle prayer and intercession. Prayer reinforces spiritual intimacy and relationship and the enemy hates for us to spend time with God. The enemy knows that during those intimate seasons of prayer, many seeds of destiny are planted within our spiritual wombs. In the natural, the result of intimacy between a husband

and wife is pregnancy; when a seed is conceived. In the Spirit, when godly seeds are planted, there is a planned spiritual birthing.

God desires to impregnate us with destiny and then empowers us to fulfill our purpose. This is the very reason satan sets his sight to dismantle prayer. The enemy sets his goal to **abort the destiny** of Christ's Bride!

Our spirit is truly willing, but our flesh can be extremely weak under pressure. The enemy knows that if he can abort prayer then he can weaken us. Prayer causes the spirit man to become strong just as the lack of prayer will strengthen the fleshly nature. We must continually watch over our spirit man, feed our spirit with the Word of God and continue to watch and pray so that the wicked one will not ensnare us.

> *And take heed to yourselves, lest at any time your hearts be over-charged with surfeiting, and drunkenness, and cares of this life, and so that day come upon you unawares.*
>
> *For as a snare shall it come on all them that dwell on the face of the whole earth.* ***Watch ye therefore, and pray always,*** *that ye may be accounted worthy to escape all these things that shall come to pass, and to stand before the Son of Man.*

Luke 21:34-36 (emphasis mine)

Using Spiritual Discernment

Binding the Strongman:
Matthew 12:29 reveals a spiritual principle given to all believers; that principle being "binding the strongman."

> *Or else how can one enter into a strong man's house, and spoil his goods, except he first **bind the strong man**? And then he will spoil his house.*

Matthew 12:29 (emphasis mine)

The word *bind* in this passage is a Greek word meaning to tie or fasten with chains[11]. In other words, in order to take spiritual authority over the *strong man* in operation our first step is to tie him up with chains. These *chains* will be words of prayer concerning our situations. We bind the enemy with revelation we receive from the Lord, and as we pray over circumstances, we fasten chains around every demon that comes against us! The enemy therefore becomes imprisoned and unable to move in any intended direction. His planned strategies are suddenly negated and we have the victory!

Just imagine, every time you pray another link is added to the chain that will bind your enemy! I pray that the chains that you are using are LOOOOOOONG chains! If your chain isn't long enough.....START PRAYING NOW!

Binding with Keys of the Kingdom:

Aren't you glad that Jesus has not left us defenseless against the enemy? Not only has He given us His name to use against satan, He also gave us the keys to the kingdom.

> *And I will give unto thee the keys of the kingdom of heaven: and whatsoever thou shalt **bind** on earth shall be bound in heaven: and whatsoever thou shalt loose on earth shall be loosed in heaven.*

> Matthew 16:19 (emphasis mine)

These keys are instruments to unlock the gates of heaven so that God's perfect will can be established on earth. Keys of divine revelation are meant to become the keys that unlock heaven's gates for breakthrough.

We are commissioned to spiritually go up into the "high places" of the Spirit with these spiritual keys of revelation and unlock doors that release spiritual breakthroughs. Every key is simply a representation of divine revelation given to us from God's own wisdom and knowledge. With divine revelation, new levels of authority will manifest. When we have received fresh revelation we are empowered to USE that revelation as a KEY for breakthrough. Until we use our keys of revelation with authority we will remain captives of satan's strategies.

Unless we continually bind the strongman, we are an easy prey. Therefore it is always important to discern the spirit in operation, during every attack of the enemy. <u>Every new assignment will require fresh discernment.</u> By using our keys, we will open doors to victory.

Satan's Seat

I have realized that there have been specific seasons when satan has gained a "seat" of authority. Yes, satan can gain a seat in our lives and a seated position over our regions and churches. This seat is a foothold of power over cities, countries, nations and individuals and any area we allow satan to rule and reign; thus becoming a throne.

Satan has a throne of authority wherever we allow sin, doubt or even unbelief. In the scriptures it speaks of satan having a seat in Pergamos (see Rev 2:1). However, we must realize that satan had a throne in not only Pergamos, but also has had his seated position over modern governments and cities as well as churches, businesses and individuals! Although satan himself cannot be in more than one place at a time, he very often releases authority to other principalities and rulers to affect nations and cities. Satan's seat of authority is often released through "territorial assignments."

Territorial Assignments

Allow me to give you an analogy of satan and his principalities having a strategy over a territory. One summer I visited my parents who lived in the country. They owned a lovely home on over 40 acres. The estate consisted of not just acreage and their personal home, but also a very nice "getaway cottage" for my needed escape times. One summer evening while we rocked back and forth in the rocking chairs and reminisced, a huge spider darted across the porch. This sudden attempt of its crossing to the other side of the back porch caught my eye. My eyes focused on this hairy, unsightly thing which appeared to be a TARANTULA! It was huge! And HAIRY! My brother-in law grabbed the nearest broom and with one swat, the spider came to a sudden halt. Relieved, I took a deep breath believing that to be the final END to this life-threatening creature! Suddenly, hundreds of baby spiders were fleeing for their lives, escaping in every direction. I couldn't believe my eyes. These baby spiders, hundreds of them, were on their mother's back before her demise. Evidently she was transporting all of her babies, and her back was the method of their transport. The spiders had piled up at least 4 spiders high; totally covering their mother's back and she ended up at least 10 times her normal size! I do not know what type of spider this was, but I felt I was witnessing something extremely disturbing. (FYI, I hate spiders!)

As I watched the tiny spiders flee in different directions, the Lord spoke to me concerning territorial spirits. Territorial spirits are set by satan over large territories, such as cities, states or regions. They are more strategic in their attempts to influence and seduce large amounts of people, even entire congregations, cities and states. An example of a territorial stronghold is the principality that Gabriel referred to as he stated to Daniel that he had encountered the Prince of Persia (see Daniel 10:20).

These *territorial strongholds*, such as the Prince of Persia, attempt to establish illegitimate satanic authority over large areas. The Lord revealed that this spider moved very similarly to a territorial demon. The larger, more powerful demons move into an area and "cover" that area with a stronghold...very similar to how a spider moves. This dark, demonic, many-legged structure hovers over its assigned area with a strategic plan to steal the life from its victims. It carries with it hundreds of smaller demons.

Once this demonic army moves into its assigned territory, the strongman releases all of the smaller demons to do their "work" upon the area. Every smaller devil has its job to do. It may be lying spirits, spirits of perversion, legalism, pornography or even a spirit of abortion. This is one way that satan gains a seat in our communities, families, governments, etc. This analogy of how satan plans territorial assignments enlightened me for future spiritual warfare. I now realize that when I take authority over territorial spirits I must discern which other demons have traveled with the main strongman. Then I go into prayer with more revelation and increased authority. Using the keys of the kingdom and divine empowerment I begin to bind the strongman.

Satan's Seat in Pergamos

Satan, in his seat of authority, plans to seduce every saint into areas of sin and apostasy to abort God's destiny for their lives. He will also do the same to affect the entire nation. Even in the local churches, satan will continually attempt to enthrone himself through strife, division, gossip, murmuring and complaining.

Obviously, where satan gains a seated position, he has a stronghold. When he had a seat in Pergamos, he had a stronghold over the entire city and God addressed the church where "satan's seat" was established (see Rev. 2:13). Pergamous was under siege by this demonic assignment, yet they had not denied their faith.

However, God had concerns against them. They upheld false doctrine, created stumbling blocks, ate foods sacrificed for idols and committed fornication (v. 14). Pergamos was rebuked for its idolatry and sin and the Lord condemned them unless they chose to repent.

The same condemnation can occur in our own lives if we allow satan to remain in his seated position. Though we may still confess Christ as our Savior and not denied our faith, very often we uphold false doctrines; false belief systems and we are stumbling blocks due to our sinful nature. If this is the case, then satan has a stronghold in our lives and churches. Unless there is repentance, we can easily become deceived; thus aborting our destiny.

Demonic Seated Positions Become Strongholds

Strongholds, put most simply, are well-fortified places in our minds that satan has influenced. If satan can defile our minds, he will influence our belief systems which in turn influence our actions. Doubt and unbelief will begin to infiltrate our faith and the results will be bondage, spiritual imprisonment and an extreme lack of victory.

I firmly believe that in most situations the battle is in the mind. This is why we are encouraged to renew our minds and cast down every imagination (from the enemy) that exalts itself against the knowledge of God. Too often, in our minds, satan has exalted his lies above God's plans and God's wisdom. By allowing an ungodly entrance into our minds we choose to believe lies spoken from the enemy. We quickly receive unchallenged words of death, lies and deceit that satan whispers into our ears. Unless we challenge the negativity, these areas become well fortified places; a stronghold of satan.

5) Casting down imaginations, and every high thing that exalteth itself against the knowledge of God, and bringing into captivity every thought to the obedience of Christ;
6) And having in a readiness to revenge all disobedience, when your obedience is fulfilled.

2 Cor. 10:5-6

When satan is able to plant his thoughts into our minds then he has gained a seated position in our lives. In situations of bitterness and unforgiveness; unless repentance is experienced and sin confessed, satan will have a seated position. Seated positions in ANY area of our hearts will therefore become places for satan to rule and reign over our lives. Some of these areas are lust and desire for position and power. Other areas could be physical lusts and perversion that we never speak of but often "think of." With the evil influences of sexual immorality promoted from Hollywood, satan has gained a stronghold, a seated position that constantly defiles our minds and thought patterns.

Strongholds of Idolatry

Every entrance allowed to satan can easily become a seated position and a stronghold. Seated places become his place to abide thus allowing him to rule and reign over us. The inhabitants of Pergamos became influenced by the idols they worshipped. First Corinthians 10:20 exposes idol worship as devil worship. The idols are nothing, but the demons behind the idols are very real. When we worship idols, the scripture states that we worship devils. In other words, wherever there is idolatry there will be a release of demonic activity. And, whatever we worship, whatever we allow to become exalted over the exaltation of God, the enemy will seat himself in that area and become empowered. If we choose to become disobedient and sinful, it opens doors of demonic oppression and activity against us.

Many Christians do not realize they are opening doors to idolatry. Idolatry is not simply bowing down to a graven image. Idolatry is choosing to believe satan's lies over God's Word. Remember saints, God and His Word are One. They cannot be separated. Believing opposite of His Word is a form of idolatry.

My 78-Pound Idol of SELF

In my early twenties I suffered from anorexia nervosa and bulimia. I battled for seven years against the lying spirit that ruled and overpowered my will to live. Satan and his cohorts had seated positions in my life. Many days I felt as if I was "driven" by demons to exhibit extreme bizarre behavior. At seventy-eight pounds, near death, the Lord began to set me free from demonic oppression. I later realized that I had been suffering the consequences of sin and idolatry. I did not actually bow down to an idol, I did not worship a Buddha or any graven image, but I did worship my body. My body image became more important than pleasing God, thus resulting in idolatry.

Eating disorders are often rooted in control issues. Like most anorexics, I wanted complete control of my life. I desperately needed to control my environment, my weight and every situation I might encounter. To prevent any perceived rejection, I remained in control through isolation. I would not leave my house for weeks except out of absolute necessity. I manipulated and maintained complete control of EVERYTHING. However, the eating disorder began to control me!

The Lord revealed to me that the anorexic thought patterns and behavior was idolatry. At first, I was shocked to realize that I was an idolater. Like many, I had mindsets that idolatry involved graven images and bowing to them. But in reality, I WAS bowing down.....I bowed low to the words of satan concerning my life.

The devil deceived me and I embraced false beliefs that God did not love me and that I was a mistake. I did not trust God and that is the reason that I decided to rule over my own life. Today, I have the full realization that the Lord desires to be my complete source. I am to depend on Him for my identity and acceptance. In the past, I chose to look to the world for acceptance and love. I felt that if I looked thin enough, I was in control. Satan uses that lie to destroy many of God's anointed. The lies attached to anorexia nervosa and bulimia are lies that steal our destiny.

"Oh, I'm not an idolater!" you might also say. "I don't bow down to ANY graven image and I am not a CONTROL FREAK!"

Please examine your heart. Are you obedient to totally follow the Lord? Do you put God first in your life? Do you spend time, quality time with Him? If other "things" or "activities" take first place, satan may have a seated position in your life just as he had in mine!

Dethroning Your Enemy

In my recent book, *Dream On*[12], I have shared my testimony of how I was equipped through dreams and visions from God to overcome death and eating disorders. The Lord commissioned me to author *Dream On* for a two -fold purpose. First, to discuss the importance of dreams and visions and activate others in dream interpretation and secondly to help them realize that God desires to deliver them from strongholds through the revelation in their dreams.

Most everyone dreams, and most likely God is speaking to each of us through dreams and visions; yet we do not recognize His voice. One of the reasons for dreams and visions is to reveal hidden patterns of behavior and generational strongholds so that we can experience freedom and deliverance. Also, as we receive levels of revelation and deliverance, satan is dethroned from his seated position in our lives!

If you are a dreamer, let me encourage you to seek information concerning God's voice. It is quite possible that even your destiny is being revealed by God speaking prophetically through your dreams!

The Church is in such transition that if we are not careful we will limit God's NEW THING. Most of us are crying out for the new wine. Though we do not wish to limit God, we still find ourselves wanting to control His Spirit. This is due to the fact that we really dislike change. We verbalize our desires for changes....but we dislike the changes that take place! And, because we are uncomfortable with the "new" we will often retreat to the "old."

Therefore, we must expect God to "break in on us" with dreams. Through godly dreams, He can by-pass the conscious mind and insert a dream, like adding a new computer chip, and speak truth to us. When we dream, we have absolutely no control...so God can speak and we cannot argue back! He will visit us in the night season and speak to us in our dreams to bypass religious mindsets.

Start paying attention to your dreams...God is speaking!

Another way to overcome a "destiny thief" is to proclaim the blood of Jesus over all sin and iniquity. Renounce the sin, re-dedicate your life to Jesus and repent for areas of defilement and uncleanness. Get back in the race and finish your course and you will develop a powerful testimony that will destroy the enemy's foothold in your life. Also, ask God to reveal any religious mindsets that block your ability to move forward with Him into your destiny and breakthrough.

Prayer:

Father God, I repent for all areas of idolatry in my life. I ask that You forgive me for being a lover of self, being selfish and self-centered. I have chosen my own way. I have chosen to follow the love of this life and the pleasures of this world over the love of Christ and His ways. I choose life this day. I choose to be an obedient vessel. Thank You for the blood of Jesus that cleanses me from all unrighteousness. Thank You for renewing my mind today. As I have repented, it removed the enemy from any seated place in my heart and life. I will continue to follow You and obey You in all my ways. I lay down my life for the sake of the gospel. I will not compromise my stand for righteousness and I will follow You all the days of my life. Empower me to remain a witness for Christ while on this earth. I use the keys of the kingdom and bind the devil and all of his plans against me in the mighty name of Jesus Christ. I choose to run my race and to finish the course You have given me. I thank You in advance for my deliverance from all oppression and evil plots against my destiny. In Jesus name, Amen.

Chapter Three

Belial

*And her adversary also provoked her sore, for to make her fret,
because the Lord had shut her womb.*

1 Samuel 1:6

She made her way to the top of the temple steps once again. Every step was an effort that day. She had not eaten for days; her sorrow and grief overrode her bodily hunger.

"Just once more," she told herself, "one more prayer to the Lord, surely Jehovah will hear me this time."

Her faith remained stable even though she still had not experienced the fruits of her hopes for a child. Year after year, she would pray in the synagogue for a son, only to return home to a later disappointment.

"Your consistent praying is a waste of time! Why do you weary yourself year after year begging your God for an offspring? God will not answer you. Haven't you realized by now that your god has shut your womb? He has turned His back on you. You will never be worthy enough to be blessed! You may as well give up this hopeless cause." This was the voice of the beguiler. It was the same voice that seduced Eve hundreds of years earlier in the garden. The lying voice became more and more familiar as she remained in her weakened, emotional condition. At times it was difficult to discern if it was the beguiler or God speaking. Hannah was worn down with grief, which made it easy for deception to become a fortress of doubt and unbelief. Her exhaustion gave way for the Accuser of the Brethren to overpower her mind. There was a definite new sound in his voice; a sudden strength of verbiage and persuasion which she could not deny …because now **Belial** was involved in the seduction. Belial had joined the teamed efforts for the total seduction of her mind, will, and emotions.

"Maybe God wants me to stop believing for a child. After all, I am one of those who never appear to get their breakthrough. I am cursed and there is no amount of prayer that will change that." Hannah's thoughts had begun to align with the enemy's overpowering voice.

"Hannah! You will NEVER have a child!" The seducing voices of Belial and the Accuser grew louder as she pressed on through into the temple.

With every step, she would hear a third voice, the one of Peninnah, her husband's second wife. Peninnah was blessed with children; Hannah was not. Though her husband, Elkahah continued to give Hannah double portions and appeared to love her greatly, it was still not enough. External attention and blessings would never satisfy the barrenness she experienced. Only the blessing of conception would bring complete fulfillment.

"I have a heritage and you don't." Peninnah's words were rehearsed in Hannah's mind. "You may receive more attention from our husband, but you will NEVER be a mother. You will NEVER experience the attention I receive, because I have given him many children."

Each recalled word from her adversary caused her more grief but with every ounce of faith she continued to pray for her miracle.

"This time will be different," she fought for the words of faith for a positive confession. "I will choose to believe that God will bless me. He will NOT leave me barren."

Uncontrollably, Hannah began to cry out loud. Finally empowered to prevail over the voice of the seducing spirit, she wailed so loudly that the priest in the temple had begun to observe her peculiar actions.

"I don't care what people think about me!" She began confessing beneath her breath. "I am going to touch God today with my prayers!" (I can easily identify with Hannah and the battle for her mind!)

"Don't get too loud, now." The sly, seductive voices whispered. "People know you will never have a child. The priest knows you will never have a child. You are wasting your time. What makes you believe God would listen to YOU?"

Oh, God! Hannah cried out within herself. Her silent prayers chose to NEVER give any place to the seductive spirits.

"If You will give me a son, I will dedicate him to You! No razor will touch his head, and I will give him to You all the days of his life." She continued to voice these vows in her heart never uttering an audible word.

Hannah was determined that she would never surrender her faith and agree with the familiar voice that tempted her to doubt her prayers. Her sorrow and lack of fulfillment were taking a back seat to her renewed faith and vision. With only her lips moving, she got the priest's full attention.

"Woman, don't you know you are not to come to the temple drunk? How long have you been praying under the influence of the wine?" Eli asked.

"Now look what you've done!" The voice of satan grew louder. "Run away! Stop your senseless praying. Now even the priests are making fun of your efforts. How can you expect God to believe your prayers? You are a worthless, cursed old woman. Good for nothing, that's what you are."

The destructive voice pounded against her mind. "You are insignificant, ruined and marked with barrenness. What makes you believe that today's prayers are any different from the rest of your senseless petitions?"

Hannah pressed through her fear of rejection. For years she had persevered beyond the cutting words from Peninnah. Living in the same household with her adversary was almost unbearable; yet she was able to reserve a portion of hope through it all. Her frailness was the result of grief due to her barren situation, having been so distraught and vexed by her adversary she was unable to eat. The familiar voice was constantly invading her faith and falsely accusing her. Yet, by the grace of God, she continued to believe God for the blessing.

"Would it be different this time? *Could* it be different this time? Will God hear me? Similar to a broken record, these thoughts replayed through Hannah's mind while Eli continued to drill her with questions and accusations.

Hannah's spirit arose within her as she continued to battle the foreboding voice of Belial. It was a wicked spirit. Even its name represented *wickedness, good for nothing and worthless.* Belial was a demonic influence that forecast and accomplished ruin and destruction upon victims that surrendered to its lies. With tremendous determination, Hannah stood strong in her faith.

"I am not drunk, only sorrowful!" Hannah firmly vindicated her actions. "I am pouring out my desires to the Lord. I am NOT wicked, nor a daughter of Belial." Her fortress of faith commanded a victory. She was persevering while holding her ground, still believing God would hear her prayers.

Eli gazed upon her countenance. Knowing this woman was touching the very heart of the Father; he blessed her. "Go in peace," he said, "The God of Israel is granting your petition." [13]

The results of Hannah's determination removed Belial from his seated position.....the spirit surrendered its stronghold and now Hannah was freed from the Accuser's stratagem.

Hannah shifted into her destiny and fruitfulness.

Wherefore it came to pass, when the time was come about after Hannah had conceived, that she bare a son, and called his name Samuel, saying, Because I have asked him of the LORD.

1 Samuel 1:20 (emphasis mine)

The Destiny Thief, Belial

Most of us, at one time or another, will face the same foe as Hannah. The biblical account of Hannah and her conflict with barrenness is documented in 1 Samuel Chapter One. It is a story of a godly woman who chose to fight in faith rather than retreat and surrender to hopelessness. Her adversary continually troubled her and provoked her to sorrow (v. 6). Many times she could have chosen to not return to the temple and pray for a son, yet she continued to believe God would answer her prayers.

Can you relate to Hannah? Many of us have been barren and unfulfilled. Multitudes of God's children have cried out to fulfill destiny only to be continually seduced and provoked to embrace doubt and unbelief. Hannah had the tenacity to press forward and continued to believe God. Battling the strongholds of Belial she remained strong while believing God for her breakthrough.

Hannah made the confession to Eli that she was NOT giving place to the spirit of Belial. Out of her own mouth she identified the evil spirit behind the seductive voice of beguilement.

> *Count not thine handmaid for a daughter of Belial: for out of the*
> *abundance of my complaint and grief have I spoken hitherto.*

1 Samuel 1:16

The voice of Belial in Hannah's era is the same voice involved in today's spiritual seduction. The name *Belial* is another name for satan translated as *wicked, ungodly, evil, worthless and good for nothing.* The name also applies to *ruin, destruction, having lack, and to wear out.*[14]

Have you been experiencing extreme weariness while endeavoring to believe God for fruitfulness? Has the enemy attempted to seduce your thought patterns as he tried with Hannah? Have you heard a beguiling voice whispering into your thoughts statements similar to these?

> You are worthless!
> You are evil and ruined!
> You are wicked and good for nothing!
> God would never answer your prayers!
> You should be ashamed of yourself!
> You would be better off dead!

If you have heard these words, then there is a seducing, beguiling, Belial spirit which is attempting to wear you out and wear you down. It is the same spirit that competed for a seat of authority in Hannah's thought patterns. The spirit of Belial is a demonic stronghold that reinforces patterns of shame. The spirit attempts to convince us that we deserve evil and that we will never "measure-up" to the expectations of others. Also, we may believe that WE are always to blame for perceived failures.

Can you imagine the pain that Hannah experienced? First, she struggled with the shame of unfruitfulness; her inabilities to give her husband a son. Secondly, the humiliation and guilt that she experienced because her husband's other wife COULD give him children made her feel even more useless and inadequate. Thirdly, something inside Hannah confirmed that it was her destiny to have a child…yet that promise was not being fulfilled.

Most likely we all identify with Hannah, believing that there is more in life than what we are experiencing. However, when a spirit of Belial is active, the shame is unbearable and the seduction of Belial's lies overwhelms our faith. A constant bombardment from the evil one wears us down and we submit to the false belief that we are worthless and that circumstances will never change.

Because Belial is so persuasive and seductive in its tactics, many may even commit suicide. The result of hopelessness has proven totally devastating causing even God's children choose death over life. Belial targets our children and suicide is at an all time high among teenagers.

We must lock into LIFE! We must CHOOSE life! There is so much to live for; especially fulfilling destiny!

Belial's Seductions

1. Idolatry
Belial is mentioned in several other passages in scripture. In Deuteronomy 13:13 it specifically mentions the children of Belial as those who are influenced by strongholds of idolatry. In this passage, the Scriptures have pointed out that those who are seduced by *Belial* have pursued others to embrace lifestyles of wickedness and idolatry. They will say, "Come with us! Go our way, and we will serve other desires!" It is similar to satan baiting a hook, tossing it in our direction while hoping we will swallow his bait!" In other words, it is another form of spiritual seduction.

> *Certain men, the children of Belial, are gone out from among you, and have withdrawn the inhabitants of their city, saying, Let us go and serve other gods, which ye have not known;*

Deut 13:13

2. Illegitimate Authority

One way Belial operates in today's churches is through a person (or a group of people) attempting to gather others unto himself/herself. These are self-proclaimed leaders who are administrating power through illegitimate authority. Because of an offense or a lack of personal recognition, they seek others to "come to their side." The strategy is to gain influence and power by falsely accusing spiritual authority, and to control and manipulate by the twisting of words in an attempt to destroy unity.

These self-proclaimed leaders guide others through doors of rebellion, serving the god of their own fleshly desires of control and power. We may not understand these methods as "idolatry" but any religious system and structure that is above the principles and character of Christ is idolatry. The Lord and His Word are One; (see John 1:1) meaning He cannot be separated from His Word. Any beliefs or practice opposite of His Word is idolatry! Therefore, Belial is another spirit of seduction that ensnares us into spiritual idolatry and harlotry.

The Lord rebukes those who heed and give a seat of authority to the destructive spirit of Belial. God is most specific in commanding that his children are to utterly destroy all that are influenced by this stronghold. God instructed Israel that if they simply were to **hear** of the inhabitants giving authority to the spirit of *Belial* they were to *utterly destroy ALL* of the inhabitants in that entire city. This is specifically instructing us to not give heed to Belial's voice or those in agreement with this spirit.

> *12) If thou shalt* ***hear*** *say in one of thy cities, which the LORD thy God hath given thee to dwell there, saying,*
>
> *13) Certain men, the children of* ***Belial***, *are gone out from among you, and have withdrawn the inhabitants of their city, saying, Let us go and serve other gods, which ye have not known;*
>
> *14) Then shalt thou enquire, and make search, and ask diligently; and, behold, if it be truth, and the thing certain, that such abomination is wrought among you;*
>
> *15) Thou shalt surely smite the inhabitants of that city with the edge of the sword, destroying it utterly, and all that is therein, and the cattle thereof, with the edge of the sword.*

Deu. 13:12-15 (emphasis mine)

The seductiveness of Belial was such a detriment to Israel that God gave specific instructions to destroy everyone who allowed Belial to remain in a seated position of authority. The commandment of destruction included destroying all the cattle as well! No evil influence of the Belial nature was to be left living. The Israelites were to take the idols and burn them with fire and destroy the city. It was forbidden for Israel to partake of the spoils. If they disobeyed and took the spoils then they were convicted of "taking cursed things" (v. 17).

For us, today, it will require the cleansing fire of the Holy Spirit to burn away the agreements made with this enemy. If we repent and turn from our wickedness, He will be faithful to cleanse and heal our land (see 2 Chronicles 7:14).

3. Homosexuality

In Judges 19:22 we notice the passage where there were *sons of Belial* who demanded sexual relationships with another man. The master of the house refused to allow his guest to be shamed in such a manner so he allowed the evil men to sexually abuse his daughter. This was such a vile thing for this man to do; however, let's carefully examine the influences of this evil spirit. The stronghold is so powerful that it can persuade a father to shame his own daughter. Also, it manifests as sexual perversion as discussed in 2 Timothy 3:1-3:

> *1) This know also, that in the last days perilous times shall come.*
> *2) For men shall be lovers of their own selves, covetous, boasters, proud, blasphemers, disobedient to parents, unthankful, unholy,*
> *3) Without natural affection, trucebreakers, false accusers, incontinent, fierce, despisers of those that are good,*
> (emphasis mine)

4. Belial and False Accusations

In 2 Samuel Chapter 20 we read where the stronghold of Belial entered into the heart of Sheba. Sheba led a rebellion against King David and as a result had to be slain (utterly destroyed) to keep peace in David's army. How many times have we witnessed the influence of Belial operating within the local church? The stronghold of rebellion is constantly manifesting in attacks against godly authority through slander, false accusations and rebellion. This spirit has to be addressed and prayed against. It must be ostracized and rendered helpless by giving it no place or authority within the Church. To preserve corporate unity in David's army, everyone in agreement with the spirit of Belial had to be destroyed. Think of this in terms of the corporate church. Discipline is necessary if there are attempts to disrupt unity or the result is spiritual and corporate defilement. So, we can conclude that Belial co-labors with and may even foster rebellion!

5. Stealing Your Inheritance

In 1 Kings 21:10 Jezebel had sons of Belial falsely testify against Naboth so that she could illegally possess his vineyard. Her husband, Ahab, was King of Israel and he strongly desired Naboth's vineyard. Naboth wanted to maintain ownership of the vineyard because it was his inheritance. One day Ahab pouted and cried to Jezebel, concerning the vineyard. Jezebel manipulated circumstances to steal the vineyard from Naboth. She had liars (influenced by Belial) to bear false witness against Naboth. As a result, Naboth was murdered and Ahab acquired the vineyard. In this passage we recognize Belial personified as satan; the lying, seducing, beguiling, unclean, murdering stronghold.

Today, we witness the same spirit falsely accusing others. The spirit is still manifesting in the identical manner of the past: seducing believers into sins of the flesh, spiritual wickedness, doubt and unbelief, sexual perversion, lies and deceit, rebellion, slander, false accusations and even murder. Obviously, Belial cohabitates with Jezebel while attempting to steal all of our inheritance, as they did to Naboth!

Saints, if you are giving any place to Belial and Jezebel, your entire future is threatened! Your intended destiny and inheritance is at risk if you allow satan to occupy a seat in your life. You must take steps to utterly destroy all! In other words, stop now and ask God to open your heart to any needed correction. Utterly destroy anything that God says displeases Him. (Also, more is mentioned on utterly destroying all in the following chapters.)

Please ask yourself this question: Have you been targeted by this seductive spirit to spread disunity? If so, repent now, and ask the Lord to cleanse your heart from any defilement, and then return to the unity of God's Word.

6. Selfishness and Self-Centeredness

As a recent pastor of a local church, I never fully understood why so many Christians remained self-centered. As believers, we should be more concerned for the welfare of others than ourselves, but all too often, godly people remain in patterns of self-centeredness and co-dependency. Because it is our destiny to win souls for Christ and to be concerned for the lost, it bothered me why many Christians remained stagnant in their concern for others. Choices were made to remain in areas of "woundedness" and "victimization" rather than reach out and minister to others in need. After I searched the scriptures, I realized that King David dealt with the same problems of self-centeredness... within his own army!

In the passage of 1 Samuel 30, King David had defeated the **Amalekites** and recovered all that the enemy had stolen from him. It was a tremendous victory. David reaped the spoils of battle and desired to share it with the rest of his troops. But, there arose a problem within his army. The scripture states that the sons of Belial did not want to share the spoils! **(Here we identify two strongholds working together; the Amalekites and Belial).**

David had left the weak soldiers behind and did not force them into battle. This was a wise decision of the leader, for he would have forfeited their lives because of their weakened condition. In the battle against the wicked Amalekites, David and his army were empowered to overtake their enemy and recover all which had been stolen! Because David's heart was unified with his people, he desired to share the victory and the spoils with everyone, (the heart of a true leader). However, Belial was at work after their great defeat of the Amalekites. Even after a great victory, the seduction of selfishness and self-centeredness, along with greed, manifested through David's men....they were referred to as the men of Belial.

> *21) And David came to the two hundred men, which were so faint that they could not follow David, whom they had made also to abide at the brook Besor: and they went forth to meet David, and to meet the people that were with him: and when David came near to the people, he saluted them.*

22) Then answered all the wicked men and <u>men of Belial</u>, of those that went with David, and said, because they went not with us, we will not give them ought of the spoil that we have recovered, save to every man his wife and his children, that they may lead them away, and depart.

1 Samuel 30:21-22 (emphasis mine)

David realized that even though some of his men were left behind, they remained a valid part of the army. The *men of Belial* were only concerned about themselves, their own sacrifices and their self-promotion.

Belial will attempt to influence others into believing that their success is due to their personal charisma and their own gifting with no thought of others who sacrificially gave in order for that leader to achieve levels of success.

7. Spiritual Barrenness

The spirit of Belial also seduces us to believe and agree with any lie, which would cancel our destiny. Belial seeks a seated position in our lives through distortions of truth and false belief systems. Its aim is to seduce us into believing the very opposite of what God has said using counterfeit words which will counteract His promises!

The spirit of Belial applies extreme pressure to wear us out. Once exhausted and vulnerable, we are forced to then give up any footing gained. As a result, the enemy will move in for the "kill." After all hope is destroyed, and all joy has departed; the vulture, satan, swoops down upon us to kill, steal and destroy.

Remember, the Word states that perilous times represent times of *violence* and *fierceness*. A vulture is fierce in its kill. It circles over and over, waiting for its prey to die, then swiftly swoops down upon its victim, sometimes before it is completely dead! A vulture will pick its victim apart, piece-by-piece until its appetite is satisfied.

When Belial fiercely attacks, we often feel dead and lifeless as vision is blocked. If we quit running the race and give up in despair, the results are more barrenness and lack of fulfillment- often ending in spiritual death.

When vision is lost or even postponed, we have not only lost hope but we can easily perish! A death assignment can gain a victory when there is a loss of

...... for destiny. In my husband's recent book, *Regaining Vision*[15], he reveals that loss of vision is similar to a ship not having a rudder. There is no definite direction, just a ship tossing to and fro by adverse waves. Like so many of us when our destiny is robbed or stolen; we are easily tossed back and forth from one wind of adversity to another with no determination to achieve or to accomplish a goal. As with Hannah, if she had permanently lost vision, she would have also lost hope to press onward. Finally, when the Word of the Lord came, she was empowered to hope once more, her vision was restored and Belial was finally defeated!

Strategies for Overcoming Belial

1. Be Determined to Fight for Your Blessings

Hannah held fast to her faith in God. Though tempted to abandon her hopes for a male child, she continued to cry out to God for her blessing. We must be determined to do the same. Hannah was much like Jacob who struggled for the blessings of God. Jacob wrestled with the angel of God until he possessed his breakthrough. In fact, he wrestled all night and refused to let go of God until he received the blessing. Can you imagine this type of determination....wrestling with the angel of the Lord? What boldness. What determination. What FAITH!

Just picture Jacob, wallowing in dirt and weeds all night long. He was most likely weary from the night's adventure, yet he chose to hold on until he received his heart's desire. He sacrificed his sleep, his energy and comfort to get the victory! Jacob had made up his mind that it was time for a change. Up to this point, he had been a liar and deceiver. In fact his name, Jacob, means "supplanter and schemer."[16] Now, all alone with no one near to help him, he meets God face to face. Jacob decided that the old is passed away, and the time had arrived for his "new thing!" That new thing he needed was a new name and the blessings of God spoken over his life. And his perseverance paid off because during that wrestling match God changed his name from Jacob, the supplanter, to Israel, the prince of God. Wow! Talk about a shift!

Hannah had a destiny and was just as determined to receive her blessing. Her destiny was to birth a son, Samuel, who was to become a mighty prophet of God. In fact, it is important to remember that her destiny was linked to her son's destiny. We are all connected in the Body of Christ. When one of us reaches our destiny, another will reach theirs. This is a good reason to pray for each other!

2. Have Faith in the God of the Possible

Yes, each of us has a destiny. We will have to fight for our breakthroughs and destiny just as Hannah and Jacob fought for their fulfillment. We each have a predetermined destiny to birth something more than what we are presently experiencing. In the natural, it may seem impossible. But it is our season as children of God to press into the supernatural realm of the possible. Our God is the God of the Possible. All things are made possible through our Lord. Though we may be barren, we must be determined to believe for the impossible to manifest as the possible.

Don't give up on your promises! Never quit believing that God will bless you. Be like Hannah and Jacob and believe God to release you from your barren situations.

> *And Jesus looking upon them saith, With men it is impossible, but not with God: for with God all things are possible.*

Mark 10:27

3. Realize That Your Strength Lies in Warfare

Your strength and your ability to defeat Belial will be in your determination to war over your inheritance! It is time for each of us to come out of the wilderness. Song of Solomon 3:6 speaks of the bride coming out of the wilderness. This is a passage of the wedding procession; the king awaiting his bride. Symbolically, it represents Jesus who awaits His bride that is finally coming out to greet Him. His bride has been prepared. Though she has been in the wilderness, (that season of her life which has cleansed and purified her in every way) she is finally COMING OUT to meet her king!

> *Who is this that cometh out of the wilderness like pillars of smoke, perfumed with myrrh and frankincense, with all powders of the merchant?*

Song of Solomon 3:6

Do you remember the biblical account of Esther and how she was mentored and "made ready" for twelve months to approach the king? The number twelve is symbolic; meaning new government. Esther was being prepared to be a queen that could change and shift government.

For a solid year she was bathed in oils and perfumes. She was purified with myrrh for six months. The number six is symbolic for flesh or the number for man. Symbolically, we can conclude that Esther was purified and cleansed from all fleshly desires and sinful nature. This was all her process of perfection; all needed to empower her to become a queen who shifts governments and institutes godly decrees.

Esther did not lavish a "Calgon-take-me-away" soaking. But rather the myrrh was SCRUBBED into her skin. Esther was not simply "oiled down" or "sprayed" with perfume like today. The fragrance became a part of her...the fragrance was scrubbed into her skin to become who she was...a sweet smelling fragrance.

Isn't this similar to what God desires in each of us as His Bride? He wants us to be that fragrance...not just a sweet smell that dissipates in a few hours. No, He will rub us with His hand to purify and cleanse us in our preparation to meet the Bridegroom.

When we study the word **anoint** it means not only smeared with grease but also "rubbed" with oil! Therefore, part of the anointing process is the rubbing and scrubbing!

Esther being rubbed and scrubbed with myrrh was extremely significant; just as it is for us today. Let's take a look at its symbolism:

- Myrrh was sacred oil used to anoint the robes of the priesthood. The priests were "set apart" and anointed as servants in God's house. (We are also "set apart" and anointed to serve as priests)
- Myrrh translates as "bitter." Esther was adopted. If there was any bitterness in her heart, due to rejection or abandonment issues, it had to be scrubbed and rubbed out so that she could come forth into her full destiny. (We must allow God to cleanse all bitterness of the past from our lives in order for us to become anointed vessels and fulfill destiny)
- Myrrh was used in burial preparation. (There must be a death to self and selfish ambition to achieve our full destiny.)

4. Be a Covenant Warrior

Behold his bed, which is Solomon's; threescore valiant men are about it, of the valiant of Israel. 8 They all hold swords, being expert in war: every man hath his sword upon his thigh because of fear in the night.

Song of Solomon 3:7-8 (emphasis mine)

In verse 7 it states that around the bed are armed men of war! Now, who would ever imagine that a King would desire armed soldiers surrounding his marriage bed? However, this passage is symbolic of the needed spiritual warfare in this season. The bed represents covenant relationship, which implies receiving our inheritance based on the covenant promises from intimacy with Christ.

The only way we will receive the covenant blessing is through warfare. Notice that it states that the sword is not drawn but rather at the thigh. Symbolically the thigh represents strength and reproduction. In other words, our strength to possess our promises and to be delivered from spiritual barrenness lies in our determination to war over our promised inheritance.

Saints, it's time for war! Don't back down! Most of us are weary of warfare, but we cannot quit fighting the enemy. Remember Caleb? He was 80 years old and still fighting! He endured the wilderness and then came out! In Caleb's desert place he was being prepared for his covenant promise. He came out of his wilderness with an increased determination to receive God's blessings and promises.

We must be like Caleb and declare, "GIVE ME MY MOUNTAIN!"

YOU ARE DESTINED FOR FRUITFULNESS!

Let's Review the Ways to Recognize Belial at work:

1. Physical attacks and weakness; being worn out
2. Generational spiritual wickedness
3. Overwhelming shame and hopelessness
4. Lies, uncontrollable thoughts of despair and failure
5. Thoughts of suicide and self-destruction
6. Recognizing a thief in your finances or losing your inheritance
7. False accusations
8. Selfishness, self-centeredness and greed
9. Lust, perversion, unclean thoughts and patterns of behavior
10. Idolatry in any form
11. Lazy, lukewarm and compromising
12. Illegitimate authority; unable to submit to and trust authority
13. Natural or spiritual barrenness
14. Negativity

How to Pray a Prayer of Deliverance and Repentance

1. As you begin to pray, first renounce any or all of the ways you have agreed with Belial's lies.
2. Ask the Lord to forgive you for each of the areas of sin.
3. Be specific in renouncing each generational pattern.
4. Ask God to forgive your ancestors and yourself for allowing Belial to have a seat of authority.
5. Choose to forgive yourself and others for the sins and consequences of the sin.
6. Renounce any ungodly beliefs that you have concerning yourself and others.
7. Break covenant with the lies of Belial that you may have come into agreement with.
8. Agree with God's Word and what He declares over your life.
9. Thank the Lord for the Blood of Jesus, which cleanses you and places you in right standing for your promised inheritance!

Chapter Four

PURGE OUT THE LEAVEN!

... Know ye not that a little leaven leaveneth the whole lump?

1 Cor 5:6b

One cup of flour, 1 teaspoon of baking powder, one-half cup of shortening and one teaspoon of soda. Mix it all together in a bowl and what do you have? Absolutely nothing but some <u>lifeless</u> ingredients. If you are hoping for bread, you need to add the yeast. Upon adding the magic ingredient of *yeast*, a multiplication process begins; suddenly we have an "<u>alive" substance!</u> Yeast is an ingredient which not only causes fermentation in wine, but it is a source of <u>reproduction.</u> The yeast actually reproduces itself through <u>agitation</u> meaning that the combination of yeast and other ingredients causes a reaction that releases the <u>multiplication</u>.

After a measure of time the combined substances become what is commonly referred to as a *lump of dough*. Now, you can take the dough, knead it several times, form a loaf, place it into the oven and after baking you will have delicious bread.

By simply adding the one single ingredient of **yeast**, the mixture will rise and form the lump; without it there is no increase or expansion within the lump to make leavened bread.

Christ used the symbol of yeast to explain how just a little amount of sin can multiply into a whole "lump" of sin. Apostle Paul addressed the Corinthians concerning their sins and said that they needed to <u>purge</u> the least amount of leaven so that the entire Church would not be seduced by the sin. Just a little leaven (yeast) will multiply quickly and before you realize it, the entire congregation is in sin. And, the more <u>agitation</u> which occurs, the more leaven is created….and the more sin will abound!

God commanded us to be fruitful and multiply (see Gen 1:22, 28). However, this is the example of positive multiplication. There are several examples of multiplication in the Scriptures. One type occurs when people pray together. Deut. 32:20 states that when one prays it puts one thousand demons to flight. But, when two pray, it puts ten thousand to flight! This is God's type of positive multiplication; an exponential increase. Another example is giving. When we give offerings to God, the Word says it is multiplied back to us (see Luke 6:38).

Obviously, if you desire expansion such as needed in making bread, this is a desired multiplication! But if it is the leaven, or the yeast, referred to in scripture as sin, then, it is an undesired result of multiplication.

The enemy is always quick to attempt a seduction; he will cause <u>agitation</u> among the sheep and then sit back and observe the results of its multiplication. If he can manifest through a saint to spread gossip and slander, then the multiplication process will begin. Gossip will be on the "rise" as yeast to flour and then soon there is an <u>entire lump of strife and division</u> formed within the Body of Christ.

Apostle Paul encouraged the believers to purge out the old leaven so that they might become a new lump and free of sin. By admonishing them to become *unleavened* they would be free of defilement, malice and wickedness.

> *6) Your glorying is not good. Know ye not that a little leaven leaveneth the whole lump?*
> *7) Purge out therefore the old leaven that ye may be a new lump, as ye are unleavened. For even Christ our passover is sacrificed for us:*

8) Therefore let us keep the feast, not with old leaven, neither with the leaven of malice and wickedness; but with the unleavened bread of sincerity and truth.

1 Corinthians 5:6-8

At the time Israel was released from Egypt, they were instructed by the Lord to eat only **unleavened** bread. During each future Passover celebration, Israel was to remember their exodus from Egypt by eating the **unleavened** bread. This was all symbolic of Israel being separated from Egypt and removed from the bondage of sin. The Red Sea crossing was symbolic of a death to the old man, and being baptized through Christ into the new life. Due to the blood sacrifice of Christ Jesus, our sins are washed away and we become new creatures.

God's Word instructs us to refrain from negative reports, association with idolaters and the filth of moral sin (yeast which multiplies).

Yeast Multiplies Through:

1. Negative Reports

As a former pastor and a present leader, I do not believe that God's children fully understand the effects of negativity and negative reports; especially how it affects a church congregation. If we fully perceived the damage that negativity had upon our destiny, we would remain positive and watch every single word uttered from our mouths! I have easily related to Moses, the Israelites pastor in the wilderness, because he saw the immediate effects of a negative report from members of his congregation.

Do you remember the example given in Numbers 13, when Moses sent the twelve spies into Canaan? Moses gave instructions to spy out the land and to study the surroundings. The task Moses gave the twelve was not to focus on the strength of the giants, but return with details of strategy to DEFEAT the giants! Moses knew there would be warfare, but the plan was not to determine IF they would take the land but rather HOW they would take the land.

By studying the strategy of Moses' commissioning, he was sending the twelve forth as a "reconnaissance team." A reconnaissance team moves into a territory, studies the natural surroundings and then sizes up the strengths of the enemy. Following those steps a plan is devised of how to overcome those strengths and make them weaknesses. There was never to be an option as to whether or not they were to go in and take the territory, but HOW they were to take it!

Moses' instructions to the spies was to study the land and determine if it was good or bad, fat or lean, wooded or barren (see Numbers 13:20). More details were required of the spies; such as evaluating the people and how many occupied Canaan. They were to report on the cities; whether they were walled or open.

The twelve quietly crossed over the Jordan and sneaked into Canaan to spy out the territory and returned after forty days. Does the number forty sound familiar? Moses was in the desert for forty years; Jesus was tested for forty days, and Noah endured the flood for forty days and nights. There are many scriptures, which refer to the number forty. This particular number is symbolic of testing. Think about this, Israel had FORTY days to overcome negativity and return with a positive attitude.

Of all the items they could have carried back for the nation of Israel to see, they chose to bring grapes…BIG grapes! (Giants eat giant grapes!) The cluster of grapes was so large they had to bear the grapes upon a staff and equalize the weight between two men. Wow! Can you imagine ordering a fruit plate for dinner that night? Just one grape would probably cover an entire plate!

I have often wondered why they chose to bring back the fruits of the land and accompany the good of the land with a negative report. They could have returned with several stones from a well-fortified wall, a description of the gates of the cities, the armor of a soldier, or a description of the hills, valleys and watering holes. Instead, they brought back FRUIT! They used wisdom by focusing on the fruit and bringing it to show the people the fruits of the land…. But as I previously mentioned they followed it with a negative report! It's like saying, "Look at this luscious fruit, look at the giant clusters, and gaze upon the ripeness of this harvest. And there is more, so much more waiting for us! BUT WE CANNOT HAVE ANY OF IT BECAUSE THERE ARE GIANTS IN THE LAND!!!

Talk about a "set up!" It sounds just like the devil and how he lies to us today. We hear messages about breakthroughs, how much God desires to increase our finances, heal us and bless us. We begin to visualize the breakthrough, we can taste the victory....then the devil speaks into our ears and says "BUT IT'S NOT FOR YOU! Don't you know that miracles died with the apostles? Don't you know you'll never be blessed?" If we choose to listen to the negative report of the enemy, we will focus on the giants that block our breakthrough and never receive our breakthroughs.

By studying the twelve spies sent by Moses into Canaan we gain understanding of how a negative report from only ten people can defile an entire nation. **The negativity of the few became the "yeast" or "leaven" that affected all of Israel.**

Joshua and Caleb returned to Moses with a positive report. These two brave spies stood before all of Israel and proclaimed that they were well able to take the land. They encouraged them to focus on the fruit and to believe the Word of the Lord.

Because the rest of Israel chose to NOT believe Joshua and Caleb's positive report, they died in the wilderness! Choosing to not believe God has its consequences. Therefore an entirely new generation of believers was raised up to cross over Jordan and possess their Promised Land.

If we choose to not rid ourselves of the leaven and utterly destroy all we may have the same results as Israel. In a church, negativity can split a congregation, discourage leaders, cause strife and division as well as steal vision. Negative words will lead to gossip and slander. Soon, murmuring and complaining will "run amuck" and rob our faith. Doubt and unbelief will manifest within a negative environment. Pastors have often become so discouraged they have left the ministry and have been replaced with a novice. How can someone with little experience fill the shoes of a seasoned quality leader? Thus, the sheep begin to scatter because they lack trust, backsliding begins and the Church remains in the wilderness.

2. Idle Words (Shut Up and March!)

35) A good man out of the good treasure of the heart bringeth forth good things: and an evil man out of the evil treasure bringeth forth evil things.

36) But I say unto you, That every idle word that men shall speak,
they shall give account thereof in the day of judgment.

Matthew 12:35-36

We must begin to watch over our words. The Scripture warns us that we will give an account for every idle word. An idle word translates as "barren" and "lazy."[17] This means that idle words are a result of our laziness in not watching over our words and also that those words are barren. When we speak forth these lazy words they will be totally <u>lifeless and unproductive</u>! As a result, the enemy will twist the words and multiply them into negativity.

Could it be possible that in order to quench any possible negativity we need to go into battle closed-mouthed? Remember when Joshua had to march around Jericho? The entire army could not talk until the final trip around the city; then finally they got to SHOUT the wall down. They had twelve trips around the entire city to get their negativity out of their system. On the thirteenth time around only a shout of victory could be released. This may be a lesson for all of us if we want an assured victory…watch what comes out of our mouths!

Through faith in God's Word and obedience we can quench the fiery darts of the enemy! The decision is up to us as believers.   In other words, when the Lord commands us to repent and turn from our wicked ways, we need to do just that! If God says to believe that we ARE able to overcome the giants that stand before us, we need to lock our faith into His promises.

So many times we are seduced into believing that our giants are too big or that we can continue in sin. We have convinced ourselves that God, in His grace and mercy, will never discipline us …even if we are disobedient. However, the Lord does chastise those He loves. The Word of God gives specific instructions that we are to set our faces like flint toward destiny and to keep our eyes on the prize (the fruit!). We are to be obedient and continue to choose life and follow the straight and narrow path.

Throughout history, the Israelites continued to choose their own way. Many scriptures have documented events when God chastised his children due to disobedience and sin. One of His specific instructions to Israel was to *UT-TERLY DESTROY ALL.* By utterly destroying all, the leaven is removed from our lives.

3. Having a Better Idea than God's

*Now go and smite Amalek, and <u>utterly destroy all</u> that they have,
and spare them not; but slay man and woman, infant and suckling,
ox and sheep, camel and ass.*

Samuel 15:3 (emphasis mine)

Saul had a better idea!

Whenever we think of the Amalekites, most often we remember the familiar
passages concerning Saul **not** "utterly destroying all." Saul was to destroy
EVERY living person, man and woman and their children, every living animal,
even destroy the sheep. But, Saul had a better idea! He spared Agag, the king of
the Amalekites along with a vast multitude of livestock.. All that Saul considered good was not *utterly destroyed* as God had commanded. Everything that
Saul considered vile and refuse was destroyed. Saul set himself in a position to
determine what "good and bad" were while not heeding to what God indicated
was clean and unclean, good and bad.

Saul was to <u>specifically</u> destroy ALL of the Amalekites and ALL of their
animals. The disobedience that Saul displayed greatly grieved God to the point
that God repented for allowing Saul to be king (see 1 Samuel 15:11). The
prophet Samuel became so grieved over Saul's actions of disobedience that he
cried unto the Lord all night. Samuel arose the next morning knowing He had to
speak forth prophetic words of rebuke and chastisement.

When Samuel confronted Saul, he realized the king's denial was his sin.
King Saul proclaimed that he had performed the commandment of the Lord.
Saul attempted to cover his sin and indicated that he had followed God's instructions. However, Samuel responded that he still heard the bleating of the sheep
and the lowing of oxen which reminded Saul that not all had been UTTERLY
DESTROYED! The prophet Samuel was obviously anointed to expose sin and
now Saul was caught "red handed" in his sin of disobedience! How could he
vindicate himself? It was obvious that he had been found out therefore how
could he retreat from this direct exposure?

Have you heard the expression "up the creek without a paddle?" Well, I believe that is where Saul felt he was when the prophet of God directly addressed his sin. Samuel did not back down from his position as a prophet, he directly addressed Saul's disobedience and Saul began to look for a paddle to go back down stream to a safer place!

4. Playing the Blame Game

Blaming others seemed like a good idea for vindication, so Saul told Samuel that THEY brought the animals from the Amalekites and THE PEOPLE spared the best of the sheep and oxen. "After all, it was for the sacrifice to God. Only the BEST deserves to be sacrificed to Him!" But the rest of the animals, Saul tried to convince Samuel, "were UTTERLY DESTROYED!"

How many times have we denied our sin or blamed others for our wrong decisions? Problems only **multiply** whenever we refuse to face reality or not accept responsibility for our sin.

I have heard many pastors minister on the subject of **denial** and have made jokes concerning the subject… we all repeat a common phrase which is "denial is NOT a river in Egypt!" (Implying "The Nile")

Denial is a term that means that we are refusing to accept responsibility for a wrong action, or refusing to believe what is true. You might recall someone in your life who denies he is wrong or refuses to recognize fault.

Saul was in denial concerning his actions for not utterly destroying all. He blamed the people and would not accept nor admit his responsibility for the actions.

Samuel confronted Saul's disobedience a second and third time, yet Saul insisted that he obeyed God's voice and answered again in the same way "…but the PEOPLE took the chief things to sacrifice to God" (see v. 21). Saul's denial required strong chastisement; therefore God removed him from his position as king.

It was only then that Saul repented for his sin. In Vs. 24 the scripture says that Saul finally admitted that he "feared the people, and obeyed THEIR voice" (my emphasis). Saul begged God's forgiveness, but the repentance came too late for God had already rent the kingdom from Saul and had given it to another person (see v. 28).

What Is Not Destroyed <u>Rises Up</u> To Destroy Us!

A reminder of the effects of leaven, if it is not destroyed it rises up and makes a lump. If sin is not utterly destroyed, it rises and makes an "unholy lump." This is why we must allow God to lay His axe to our unholy root systems. If we don't embrace the fire of His purity, our sin will rise up and destroy us.

Remember when God instructed Saul to utterly destroy ALL?

The reason being, God knew that if the Amalekites were not totally destroyed, they would rise up at a later date and destroy Israel.

Years after Saul's disobedience concerning the Amalekites where he should have utterly destroyed them all, it was an Amalekite who took Saul's crown. Yes, the undestroyed leaven eventually rose up to defeat Saul. Yes, the leaven that is not destroyed will eventually become a <u>seat of satan</u> in our lives.

In Saul's final battle, he fell upon his own sword and it was an Amalekite who witnessed his death and took Saul's valuables. Since the crown was most likely valuable and jeweled, it was probably taken as well. Later, the Amalekite thief informed King David of the tragic death of Saul, thinking David would be pleased. But King David was very discerning and had the Amalekite destroyed. (See Samuel 1:1-16).

We must become as King David, very <u>discerning</u> and destroy every Amalekite spirit that stands in our way. Saul's example illustrates the results of disobedience; our own disobedience in refusing to destroy all unclean areas of the flesh could culminate in our own future destruction.

Unholy Alliance

We must never make any <u>alliance</u> with the devil. Saul compromised and made an alliance with the king of the Amalekites and his destiny was aborted. From the time of the compromise, barrenness was put in motion. **The results of disobedience and rebellion are always barrenness.** It is a spiritual principle that we must be obedient in order to eat the fruit of the land. Our adversary is a liar and the father of all lies. We must be like David who was discerning at all times and destroyed the strongman in operation.

Choices Determine Destiny

I have often wondered how Saul's history would have changed if only he would have chosen obedience.   How would the Bible read concerning Saul if only he had chosen to utterly destroy all? How would the history of Israel have changed if the king had chosen obedience over sacrifice?   On the same note, how would our history have changed if in the past we had chosen obedience? Our future, just as Saul's, is determined by past obedience.

Destiny in many cases is the result of past choices. Many times it is not God's choice, his very best, that we are walking through, but rather the results of bad choices. However, the Lord says that if we repent He will forgive us and keep us on paths of righteousness to insure future victories over our enemies. God promises to cleanse us from all our sins and use apparent defeats for our good! Hallelujah! If you feel that you have made the wrong choices, simply repent now! Ask the Lord to reveal any leaven and repent for any ungodly multiplication.

List below areas where there is leaven:
1.
2.
3.

Do you recognize patterns of ungodly multiplication; such as lies leading to more lies, lust leading to adultery, or as pornography leading to sexual addictions? If yes, list below:
1.
2.
3.

It's Alive! It's Alive!

Both positive and negative yeast are active and alive. Is the yeast of sin active and alive in your life right now? Dear Ones, there is a more active and higher power!

The Word of God is alive and full of power! It will cut through hidden thoughts and heart issues and expose who we really are.

> *For the word of God is full of **living power**. It is sharper than the sharpest knife, <u>cutting deep</u> into our innermost thoughts and desires. It <u>exposes</u> us for what we really are.*[18]

Hebrews 4:12 (emphasis mine)

Allow this "living" power to become "alive" within your heart and life. Repent for all hidden sin and iniquity and His Word will deliver you from all oppression and yokes of bondage. As a result <u>you will be increased in God!</u>

<u>But the word of God grew and multiplied.</u>   Acts 12:24

Some Considerations for an Assured Victory

No Leaven = Open Heaven

N ever compromise
O pen your heart to receive truth at all times

L eave denial at the Jordan
E very battle should be devoted to the Lord
A ccept responsibility for your sins and then repent
V ow that you will utterly destroy all and keep your vow
E ach time of breakthrough, give the glory to God
N egativity multiplies into more negativity

Chapter Five

THE SEDUCING AMALEKITE SPIRIT

Now go and smite Amalek, and utterly destroy all that they have, and spare them not; but slay both man and woman, infant and suckling, ox and sheep, camel and ass.

1 Samuel 15:3

"I've lost my anointing! What am I going to do now?" Ann was crying hysterically. "Now when I minister there is no life in my words. When I sing the words seem to fall to the ground. My life is in the anointing and now it is gone!"

It was true. The anointing, which was upon her life, was diminishing. My heart was sad. What could I say at this point? My thoughts went back three years...when I first met her. She came to the ministry for counsel because her life was in shambles. Ann's lifestyle of sexual perversion and drug abuse had opened doors to uncontrollable mental torment. Because the enemy had such a firm grip upon her emotions, she was battling thoughts of suicide.

I remember the first time I saw her walk through the threshold of our church building. Even through her tormented countenance I could recognize an anointing upon her life. It was one of the strongest anointings I have discerned; she was definitely "chosen."

Within a few days, she joined our ministry. She stated that she felt the presence of God and knew that she had finally found her place. During our first counseling session I explained to Ann the importance of her commitment to locking into her destiny. I began encouraging her to submit to deliverance and biblical counseling to insure a strong foundation. Her determination for freedom charted her destiny course.

Two years passed. She had experienced great levels of deliverance from demonic oppression. Her countenance took on a new "glow" and she had developed a beautiful sparkling smile.   Ann stood straight; holding her head high…the shame of her past had departed. She became one of our worship leaders and when she sang the anointing would charge the atmosphere. I was so proud of her determination to be free that I gave her responsibilities of leadership.

Then Ann began to go backwards. She met a young man whom she declared had "swept her off her feet."

I saw the enemy's strategy from afar and called her for a counseling session. During the hours together, we discussed her previous patterns of sexual deviation, bondage and past defilement.   With warnings of backsliding I coached her through lustful temptations that might arise.

I still remember Ann's words. "I know, I know," she was trying to assure me; "You don't need to worry. I will NEVER go back to that lifestyle again. The anointing is too precious to me. Besides, he's a Christian." I remember thinking how so many Christians make that very statement only to end up in sexual defilement.

Periodically I would have Ann check in, just to reassure me that she was still on the right track with the Lord. She would commit to time together and then within a few days cancel the sessions. She continued in her new relationship and I remained in prayer for her. I began to notice that she was not attending church services. At other times, she would appear through the door of the church to assist in leading worship and then suddenly exit from the building.

When I approached her concerning her commitment she shrugged off the responsibility due to her dating schedule. It was definitely apparent that this relationship was more important than her ministry.

I wanted Ann to be happy and find fulfillment in a relationship. I tried to convince her that my concern was that she would backslide into sin and therefore not fulfill her destiny. She on the other hand disregarded any concern and labeled it all as control. Her entire countenance began to change along with her attitude.

When Ann did appear to lead worship, I began to notice her lack of anointing. Little by little, the life in her smile and countenance was dying...and worst of all the anointing almost completely diminished. It reminded me of Saul. Because he did not utterly destroy all that God commanded, his entire destiny was aborted.

I made one last attempt to minister to her. "Remember the story of Saul and how God instructed him to SMITE Amalek? You've got to utterly destroy all...don't go back to an old lifestyle."

"Yes, Pastor," she rolled her eyes and spoke sarcastically, "I know what you're trying to say...but I'm NOT sleeping with him!" My discernment spoke loudly and I was certain she was not telling me the truth.

Finally I had to let go and trust that God would protect her. I grew increasingly concerned for our worship team because I knew well the effects of "a little leaven." Sexual sin on any church team opens the door wide to the enemy.

A few Sundays later I noticed disunity among the entire worship team. They were unable to agree on songs, the sound system could not be perfected, they were disrespectful to the worship leader and she especially was disagreeable. Worship became difficult to press through and we were unable, as a congregation, to fully enter into God's presence. It was now obvious. The seducing spirit had gained its entrance and now the congregation was effected. The leaven had multiplied.

I grieved the morning she opened her mouth to sing and she couldn't sing a note! Ann's voice struggled to find the proper pitch, her voice was scratchy....then she forgot her words. In a total panic, she ran off the platform and rushed into the hallway. I followed her and found her crying hysterically.

Ann knew the anointing had diminished and WHY it had left. "I've lost the anointing and the anointing is my life!" She began to sob hysterically.

I tried to comfort her. I made many attempts to counsel her. There was no response. I have not seen Ann since that day.

Though these experiences did not actually involve me, the incidences were a true account. I have documented the conversation with permission from a pastor friend to benefit others. (The name has been changed for her protection.) Even though I was not directly involved, I can identify with this struggle and I must sadly testify that it is a common story I hear quite often. Though each situation has been unique, the stronghold was always the same.

It is important to discern which spirit we battle when destiny is aborted. The *destiny thief*, **the Amalekite**, is responsible for the compromising attitude that states "I do not have to utterly destroy all...I will not smite my enemy!" Choosing to NOT utterly destroy can abort destiny. In the previous story, the Amalekite stronghold convinced this lady to compromise her morals and not utterly destroy all the leaven; leading to a multiplication of sin and rebellion.

By observing Ann's life we can identify the strategies of the Amalekite against each of us:

1. The seducing spirit targets us

2. We are seduced, opening the door to the spirit

3. We are now in sin

4. We give the enemy a seated position in our lives

5. The spirit gains a STRONGHOLD

6. We begin to backslide

7. We begin to compromise

8. Multiplied defilement occurs

9. Our destiny is aborted

Saul was also seduced by the Amalekite stronghold. He chose NOT to smite his enemy, just as Ann did. If we are not careful, the seducing spirit will do the same to us!

The word *"smite"* means to strike, beat, or kill.[19] If we do not slay (kill and utterly destroy) every trace of an Amalekite stronghold, we will find ourselves backsliding with compromise just as King Saul did.

> *"For if ye live after the flesh, ye shall die: but if ye through the Spirit do mortify the deeds of the body, ye shall live."*

> Romans 8:13

Let's put two and two together here. When God is commanding us to "get out the leaven" and to "utterly destroy all" we are immediately tempted to compromise and retain the best part. Oh yes, we might get rid of a few sins...but we will most likely hold on to the sin we enjoy the most. When there is a strong seduction of compromise...LOOK FOR THE AMALEKITES!

Disobedience, Rebellion and Witchcraft

When reading about King Saul, did you ever notice his "bad attitude?" He was prideful and rebellious. God was so upset with him that He said that his attitude and rebellion was equal to **witchcraft and idolatry**!

Obviously, as previously discussed, Saul lacked an important key needed for God's blessing; obedience! Our obedience to God's Word releases blessings upon our lives. The Twenty-Eighth Chapter of Deuteronomy is what many ministers refer to as the Chapter of Blessings and Curses. In that chapter of the Bible, the Lord lists twenty-one blessings that result in our obedience. However, also listed are fifteen curses upon children and material prosperity and over fifty curses of sickness, crop failures, war, captivity, business failure, defeat, persecution and insanity. The fruits of obedience are fruitfulness in every area and the fruits of disobedience are barrenness. Barrenness means that there is no fruit, no conception of God's Word and little hope for the future. If we allow the enemy to seduce us into rebellion and stubbornness, then we will reap barrenness and curses.

By examining 1 Samuel 15:23, we are able to identify the strategy of another *destiny thief*. Saul was rebellious and stubborn and therefore he was rejected as king...his destiny to remain king was stolen.

> *For **rebellion** is as the sin of **witchcraft**, and **stubbornness** is as iniquity and **idolatry**. Because thou hast rejected the word of the LORD, he hath also rejected thee from being king.*
>
> (emphasis mine)

It is necessary to understand that there was a stronghold in operation when Saul battled the Amalekites. The demonic influence from the Amalekites infected and influenced Saul's own life and motives. The same spirit that affected the Amalekites also began to affect Saul, therefore influencing him to become rebellious and stubborn!

As a result, God equated this sin as witchcraft. Witchcraft is a form of control and manipulation. Witches control through soulish prayers and incantations. God recognized Saul's desire to control and manipulate; therefore, he called his rebellion witchcraft!

Saints just think of this! If we are disobedient and rebellious, God refers to this as witchcraft. *When considering witchcraft! We most often envision a witch on a broom. However, God states that if we are rebellious and stubborn we have committed sins of witchcraft and idolatry!*

When we study spiritual warfare, we realize that territorial spirits in certain areas and cities are satanically designed and intended to seduce us and adversely affect us. When Paul went to Corinth, he was influenced by the spirits that operated within the city. The demonic seat was due to the extreme idol worship in the territory. The same happens to us today as we travel into different states and regions. Whatever spirit is seated in that territory will attempt to pervert God's perfect will for our lives.

For instance, if you visit areas of New Orleans, you can be affected by strong witchcraft assignments due to the extreme voodoo worship in the area. Many have reported infirmities and mind-binding spirits attacking them after being in New Orleans. I have personally driven into the area and upon entering the city discern the spiritual darkness in operation.

Please realize that when we travel to different regions, the idols worshipped in that region have demons behind them! And those demons are empowered to negatively affect our lives and minds. It was the same with Saul. When he battled the Amalekites, the same spirit that caused the Amalekites to be ungodly and defiled attempted to enlist Saul to its side!

Hopefully, Saul was attempting to be obedient to God. He at least *thought* about destroying all....but became defiled in his actions as the Amalekites seduced him to not utterly destroy all! The demonic spirits controlling the Amalekites influenced Saul when he began to possess the land. Once again, the scripture speaks of the demons in back of the idols, meaning that where there is idolatry, there are demons. Since the Amalekites worshipped idols, there was much demonic activity.

When we attempt to gain victory over strongholds in our lives, we will also have contact with powers of darkness. Have you realized that when you attempt to fast that you come up against a spirit that tries to convince you that fasting is not necessary? The voice of the evil spirit may sound something like this:

> *Don't you know that fasting is Old Testament?*
> *Jesus never commanded His disciples to fast.*
> *Fasting is dangerous; you could die from starvation!*
> *Fasting is legalism.*

Or, when you attempt a fast, every minute of your day is consumed with the thoughts of cake, ice cream and multitudes of sugar-laden delicacies. Fleshly cravings can rule, but also there are demons at work tempting you to quit your fast. Remember, satan tempted Jesus while He was fasting, he will most likely tempt you also.

Preying upon your weakness

The Amalekites were notorious for preying upon the weak and feeble. Therefore, the enemy waits for any opportune moment to catch you in your point of weakness and steal your birthright by seducing you into apostasy. He will wait until your flesh is weak, and then entice you to sin and seduce you to totally "sell out" your inheritance!

Maybe the enemy is not tempting you with fleshly desires, but the Lord is speaking to you concerning the renewing of your mind. In an attempt to gain victory over impure thoughts, every demon in hell will whisper ugly, defiling thoughts to your mind. The demons will swarm from the woodwork when you are cleansing your mind. Quite possibly you will battle, day after day, unclean spirits that will attempt to seduce you into old behaviors.

Saul battled the spirit of the Amalekites and therefore could NOT utterly destroy them. That in itself tells us that when we battle an Amalekite stronghold that there is a spirit of compromise, disobedience and rebellion that attacks us. That defiling spirit will wear us down so that we cannot UTTERLY DESTROY what God has commanded. We could easily find ourselves as Saul, being rebellious, stubborn and in denial of our sins.

Let's very carefully observe once again the events that took place in Saul's life so that we can discern how the Amalekite spirit operates. Through studying First Samuel 15, we notice these areas:

Saul was instructed to:
1. Smite Amalek
2. To utterly destroy ALL that they had
3. Spare them not
4. Slay both man and woman, infant and suckling, ox and sheep, camel and donkey

Saul's response to God's instructions:
1. Saul took Agag the king of the Amalekites alive and destroyed all of the people
2. Spared the best of the sheep and of the oxen and of the fatlings and the lambs and all that was good
3. Would not utterly destroy them

Saul's reasoning for disobedience:
1. Denial of sin: "the people made me do it!"
2. Fear of man. He feared the people and obeyed their voice.

Since Saul was battling the Amalekites during his disobedience, we can discern that the spirit among the Amalekites seduced Saul into areas of disobedience. The Amalekite spirit that prevailed in the city was strong enough to seduce the king of Israel into denial of his actions and rebellion against God's commandments. Saul made a covenant with this ungodly spirit and as a result he did not utterly destroy the **accursed things**. Therefore we must understand that when an Amalekite spirit is attacking today's churches and leaders, we are tempted to be rebellious, disobedient, prideful and in denial of our sin. Saints, it is time to go to war against the Amalekite stronghold that has held us captive. This lying spirit of compromise and rebellion has seduced our cities and regions.

The Accursed Things

Accursed things are items cursed by God. He specifically told Israel that they were not to take certain spoils from battle, yet when they did a curse would come upon them. Saul took items that he was instructed to destroy. On the same note, when WE take into our lives beliefs, items, or wickedness that God has cursed, we ourselves become cursed. In other words we are either blessed or cursed. In Deuteronomy 28 we find the list of blessings and curses. To put it simply, we are blessed by God if we obey him and cursed if we choose to disobey. If God speaks to us and commands that we are to **utterly destroy all**, then we are not to embrace an old sinful nature…but utterly destroy every area in our lives, which are displeasing to God.

Saul's destiny of happiness, life and victory was cursed and aborted due to disobedience. We can just as easily be seduced into the same compromise if we are not spiritually alert especially today.

The devil is a liar and a deceiver. John 8:44 says that he is the father of ALL lies. Satan worked through the Amalekites, a tribe rooted in idolatry, and seduced Saul to spare what was commanded for destruction. The devil does the same with us. So often he speaks into our ears with a sly, seductive voice. The voice may say:

"You don't have to stop that sin, God loves you. You are under grace and not the law. If you continue to sin, God will forgive you."

"You don't need to tithe; God doesn't need your money."

"Tithing is Old Testament. God doesn't expect you to tithe in today's church."

"You don't need to heed the Word of the Lord. After all, even if you sin, God will forgive you."

"Did God REALLY say that? It was probably your imagination or a false prophecy."

Saul decided himself what should be spared.   Don't you know that once Saul set his feet on Amalekite territory, the devil immediately bombarded his mind challenging him to negate the Word of the Lord?   He convinced Saul that God didn't mean to destroy EVERYTHING.... surely he could save the BEST, right?   In other words, satan convinced Saul (as he also does with us at times) that God really didn't know what was best!

"Hath God said?"   It has been a statement that the enemy has used since the beginning of time.   As soon as Adam and Eve were created, the snake in the garden came up with the original term: "Hath God (really) said?"   Satan said that to Eve and he is still saying it today..."Did God really say that?   Do you REALLY believe you can be healed?   Do you REALLY believe that God wants you to prosper?"   Have you heard that voice before?   The devil would like to seduce all of us into doubting what God has said!

The Money Thing!

Well, what about the money thing?   Did you know that money is neutral?   Money has no power, but money becomes evil when the spirit of mammon affects how we use our money and how we view the power of money.   When the Amalekite spirit is influencing a city, greed and power is at an accelerated high.   Drugs and crime are at peak performance because of the money made in illegal exchanges.   When people "take" money from illegal sources it is the same sin Achan committed when he took of the accursed thing!   This type of behavior results in a curse over the entire city until the curse is broken through prayers of repentance and intercession.

The scripture says that Achan "saw" and "took."   We must pray that we are not seduced by the evil of this world, partake of sin, and attempt to keep the sin hidden.

Achan's Disobedience at Ai

The defeat at Ai was the result of one man's disobedience concerning the accursed things.   God declared that all of the spoils of Jericho were devoted to Him.   However, Achan decided to take the devoted things and hide them in his tent.   As a result, a curse came upon the entire army of Israel, which resulted in the military defeat at Ai. Joshua sought the Lord and He revealed that there was sin in the camp. One person, an Israelite, had taken the devoted spoils unto himself!

When Joshua confronted Achan, he confessed his sin. Achan paid an extremely high penalty for disobedience, yet it was through his own lustful desires that he took things that God instructed to leave alone. There are times that God speaks to us and demands that we leave certain areas alone. For instance, in Leviticus 7:21 God instructed his children to "touch not the unclean thing."

Touch Not the Unclean Thing...

> *Moreover the soul that shall touch any unclean thing, as the uncleanness of man, or any unclean beast, or any abominable unclean thing, and eat of the flesh of the sacrifice of peace offerings, which pertain unto the LORD, even that soul shall be cut off from his people.*
>
> Leviticus 7:21

When the phrase *unclean thing* is translated from Hebrew, it means polluted, defiled and impure. It also translates as "to be defiled by idolatry" or "defiled sexually." The Lord foresaw that the Israelites would be tempted to intermarry with unbelievers, therefore resulting in spiritual defilement. God also foresaw that the Israelites would make ungodly covenants (sexual relations) with the women and eventually be seduced to worship their false gods; thus being defiled with the sin of idolatry. One reason why God warned Israel numerous times against intermarriage with unlike believers was because they were so easily seduced into the sins of idolatry. This is why the Lord so often demanded that Israel was to **utterly destroy all** whenever they took a city. Saul was specifically warned to not take of anything the Amalekites possessed; Joshua gave the same instructions to his army in Canaan. In fact, through Scripture we find passages where God commanded His army to utterly destroy all and to touch not the unclean things.

The Devil Carries a Suitcase!

Whenever we allow defilement and refuse to put sin under our feet and keep it there, the sin will eventually rise up against us. Its aim is for totally defeat. As I pointed out before concerning sin, Jesus said that a little leaven leavened the entire lump. I have found this to be true because if we ask the devil to dinner, he will bring his suitcase. The devil wants to MOVE IN and STAY! We are instructed to separate ourselves from sin and the worldly pleasures that attempt to seduce us into ungodly behavior.

> *Wherefore come out from among them, and be ye separate, saith the Lord, and touch not the unclean thing; and I will receive you, And will be a Father unto you, and ye shall be my sons and daughters, saith the Lord Almighty.*

2 Cor. 6:17-18

Like Saul-Like Achan

"Utterly Destroy ALL!" Many years earlier, the Lord said the very same to Saul. Saul was commanded to separate himself from the lusts of his own flesh. Saul *saw* and *took* of the best. Achan *saw, coveted* and *took* and therefore brought a curse upon the entire tribe of Israel.

> *20) And Achan answered Joshua, and said, Indeed I have sinned against the LORD God of Israel, and thus and thus have I done:*
> *21) When I <u>saw</u> among the spoils a goodly Babylonish garment, and two hundred shekels of silver, and a wedge of gold of fifty shekels weight, then I <u>coveted</u> them, and <u>took</u> them; and, behold, they are hid in the earth in the midst of my tent, and the silver under it.*

(Joshua 7:20-21)

When Saul disobeyed by not ***utterly destroying*** all of the Amalekites, Israel was destined to continue fighting them for years to come. Please remember this, our fulfillment of God's planned destiny will always affect others; it affects generations to come. If we do not utterly destroy all, then our generations will have to battle the same strongholds…sometimes at greater intensity!

If Saul had been obedient and destroyed the Amalekites, it would have saved Israel many future battles. The Amalekites thereafter continually rose up against Israel and became one of their worse enemies! The same holds true with every one of us as believers. When we are not determined to destroy sin then eventually, every area of sin that is allowed to remain will rise up to defeat us over and over and over.

The spiritual dynamics are the same in every church. We are called *out* of darkness and into His marvelous light. The commandment to walk in the light of Christ is given to *every* believer, leader and potential leaders. We are all to be separated unto Him, walking in purity and holiness and **touching not the unclean things.**

Chapter Six

AARON AND HUR, WHERE ARE YOU?

But Moses' hands were heavy; and they took a stone, and put it under him, and he sat thereon; and Aaron and Hur stayed up his hands, the one on the one side, and the other on the other side; and his hands were steady until the going down of the sun

Ex 17:12

The atmosphere was energized with God's presence. Some saints were on their faces, worshipping the Lord. Others were beginning to gather at the altar and embrace each other in love. The worship leader was caught away in a place of glory, strumming his guitar and releasing the sounds of God's presence.

I turned to my husband, Mickey, "This is wonderful," I whispered. "God's presence is so strong; don't you love the faithfulness of God?"

A loud noise rang through my ears, arresting my attention.

A man seemed to be screaming and yet at the same time weeping uncontrollably. At first, I thought it was the result of being in God's presence and that the Lord was healing the person's heart and at the same time deliverance was occurring. Then, as I looked, I realized it was the pastor of the church who seemed to be weeping not because of God's presence but from something that was devastating! I quickly discerned that something was terribly wrong with this pastor and my heart became heavy with a desire to minister life to him. I pondered over what to do. I heard the Lord say "Go over and encourage the pastor; his leaders have left him. He is very wounded and needs encouragement."

I told my husband what the Lord spoke to me and we both left our seats immediately and went to minister to the pastor. As we embraced him, he wept so uncontrollably that he fell to the floor. The Lord spoke to me that the pastor was emotionally and physically exhausted. He had been in a great spiritual battle. His leaders had abandoned he and his wife. Now he was extremely discouraged and weak. Mickey and I began to pray over him and soon he was able to stand and walk to his office.

We followed him down the corridors to his private office. Shutting the door behind him, he wept even more. Mickey and I became more concerned and offered to continue to pray for him. The pastor made his way to his desk. He sat, cupped his face into his hands and sobbed uncontrollably once more. "I cannot go on; I just cannot take another step! I have no one left to hold up my arms. If I don't have help, I cannot keep going."

My heart sank. I knew well the effect of the Amalekite stronghold for it is the spirit which attacks the "Aarons and Hurs." We had often felt as if we were in the same place as this pastor. I began to recall my own spiritual battles; times when I felt that I had no strength to remain in the race and fulfill destiny. Many times we felt as this man of God did; betrayed, helpless, suffering from loss of vision, with few dedicated people to hold up our arms and serve. "God," I cried out within myself, "help me to encourage this pastor to remain in the race!"

We tried to encourage him; we prayed with him, we counseled him - one thing was certain; he needed help - real bodies to help!

When I travel to other churches, it seems as if I hear the same complaints from senior leaders....*There are not enough servants in the House of God.* As a result, there are only a few who carry the entire load. I have realized that this is no coincidence, but rather a <u>well planned strategy of satan</u> to wear out the saints. The strategy of destroying the Aarons and Hurs, those who hold up the arms of the leaders, began with Moses and his battle with the AMALEKITES.

The Amalekites <u>AGAIN!</u>

In the previous chapter, we studied the influence of the Amalekite stronghold and how it affected King Saul and how that spirit seduces God's children into not utterly destroying all. Under its influence, we attempt to hold onto "the best" of what makes us "feel good" and not completely consecrate our hearts and minds to God. It is the stronghold that encourages us to remain disobedient and continue to embrace sin and compromise. Like King Saul there are areas in our lives we will desire to save as we commit to move forward in our relationship with God.

However, the Amalekite spirit affects us in many more areas of our spiritual walk. The spirit will not only dictate our pace of growth, but also attempts to abort destiny. Not only will this stronghold affect OUR personal destiny, but it also targets CORPORATE destiny and breakthrough. Let's continue to examine the Amalekite spirit even more closely so that we can disentangle ourselves from its evil web of destruction.

Throughout biblical history, the Amalekites were well known for preying upon the weak and feeble. This evil confederacy would remain alert, equipped and prepared to assault individuals or straggling families who slowly and feebly lagged behind a transient camp. Their tactics were to either kill the stragglers and take the spoils or seize them as slaves. Think of it...the cloud of glory would guide the camp of Israel by night and the pillar of fire led during the day. If there were any weak and feeble moving too slowly, the Amalekites would move in for the kill. Today, satan uses the same warfare tactics against us.

God is moving His Church to new levels of glory. Some decide to remain weak Christians. They choose spiritual immaturity over growth; they are feeble in their walk with God. Therefore, they lag behind with their negativity, doubt and unbelief. Or, those who have labored endlessly caring for the flock become exceedingly weary and feeble....and consequently are moving slowly out of sheer exhaustion. They have no strength to fight, which makes them an easy prey. The enemy lingers in the darkness, waiting until the right moment. Then, when we are separated from the camp, he authorizes destruction. To insure a victory, he has executed a well-planned strategy to weaken us. Satan is committed to his task and very seldom backs off easily. He does his job well, for his purpose is to speak out against the purposes of God (speaking lies to us) and to wear out the saints of God.

> *And he shall speak great words against the most High, and shall wear out the saints of the most High, and think to change times and laws: and they shall be given into his hand until a time and times and the dividing of time.*

Daniel 7:25

It's Time for a Name Change

The word Amalekite is a Hebrew word which is a derivative of a root word meaning "desperately wicked and incurable sickness." In biblical times there was a significant importance on the giving of names. Often parents would name their children prophetically, meaning they would pronounce a destiny over the child through assigning a name (title). In the case of Rachael, Benjamin's mother (Genesis 35:18), while dying during hard labor, she announced that her son would be named *Benoni* which means she named him son of my sorrow. It was not a prophetic name of who he was to become, but rather a name given out of her personal pain. However, Jacob, the father, renamed him prophetically, declaring that the son's name would be Benjamin, which means son of his right hand. In biblical times when the father placed the right hand on the son, it represented the passing of the family blessing.

Jacob fully understood the importance of a prophetic name. His own name meant *supplanter* and *deceiver*; both accurate descriptions of his character that he prophetically fulfilled. Years later Jacob experienced a name change, but at the time of Benjamin's birth, Jacob had most likely already received revelation concerning prophetic names. Rachael had named him after her own sorrow, but then the father stepped in and proclaimed a greater destiny over the son and pronounced him to be one that was "blessed."

The same holds true for each of us. So many of us were given names based on how someone else perceived us. We are often the brunt of other people's pain and their own inability to cope with life. Out of their own emptiness, many parents may have lashed out against their children with names like stupid, dumb, useless, worthless and ridiculous. These are also names that the devil feeds into our mind. Many of us have believed so many lies from the devil that we believe those lies are our name. Many times the adversary has told us that we are defeated, are worthless and are failures; we received those names and identified with them.

There may have been times of great sorrow and pain, and we have held onto old names concerning our past. We continued to wear our old garments, which reflect past behavior and character because we have been deceived to believe that it is "who we are."

But, our Heavenly Father steps in and changes our name. He renames us according to our destiny! Though we were once cursed, He promised to restore! The Word says that we are blessed and not cursed and it cannot be reversed! We have the shout of the King and therefore we can stand strong knowing who we truly are in Christ!

> *Behold, I have received commandment to bless: and he hath blessed; and I cannot reverse it. 21 He hath not beheld iniquity in Jacob, neither hath he seen perverseness in Israel: the LORD his God is with him, and the shout of a king is among them.*

Numbers 23:20-21

It is the Amalekite stronghold, which will attempt to seduce us to believe the lie that we are nothing more than worthless, helpless and defeated. But the Word over those barren, unfruitful places in our lives is that we will be fruitful and bear much fruit! Hallelujah, we can also experience a name change as did Abraham, Sarah, Jacob, Joshua, Saul and Peter!

Abraham's name was changed from Abram (father) to Abraham (father of many nations). Sarah's name was changed from Sarai (princess) to Sarah (noble woman). Both Abraham and Sarah moved forth from their place of barrenness into a destiny of fruitfulness when God changed their name. When God renamed them, it was a prophetic declaration of destiny and purpose. Not only were they to fulfill God's purpose for their lives through a name change, but also it was the way God blessed them. In each situation where God changed a name, fruitfulness was promised. Name changes can be expected when we are born again! It is a fulfillment of His covenant with each of us to be "renamed" by the Spirit. God wants us fulfilled, blessed and experiencing purpose and destiny. We can believe for change and transformation along with blessings because He is a God who does not lie and fulfills His covenant with His chosen people!

Aaron and Hur, Are You Locked Into Your Past?

The Amalekite will strategize against the Aarons and Hurs with lies that they will never experience a name change. Satan is a master deceiver and a liar and he will falsely accuse the servants of God convincing them that they are unworthy and unneeded in the House of God. However, if God will come through for those like Jacob (a liar and deceiver) and Saul (a murderer), He will also heal our hearts and change our names.

> As for me, behold, my **covenant** is with thee, and thou shalt be a father of many nations. Neither shall thy name any more be called Abram, but thy name shall be Abraham; for a father of many nations have I made thee. And I will make thee exceeding **fruitful**, and I will make nations of thee, and kings shall come out of thee.

Gen 17:4-6 (emphasis mine)

> And God said unto Abraham, As for Sarai thy wife, thou shalt not call her name Sarai, but Sarah shall her name be. 16) And I will **bless** her, and give thee a son also of her: yea, I will **bless** her, and she shall be a mother of nations; kings of people shall be of her.

Genesis 17:15-16 (emphasis mine)

We previously discussed Jacob's name change, remembering that His original name meant supplanter and deceiver. However, in Jacob's later years, when he had finally come to an end of himself, while all alone and facing one of the largest challenges in life, he became determined to change. Once again, Jacob needed to shift into transformation. Years after he had deceived his brother for the birthright, he was being confronted with his past. It was time to face his brother from whom he had once stolen and had deceived. Jacob had betrayed his family and as a thief ran off with the blessings. Now, he found himself alone with God, facing the future with an "old name." Jacob knew he could go no further without laying hold of his covenant with God. The results of Jacob's determination led to an all night wrestling match with the angel of the Lord. The final bell of the match announced Jacob's name change from Jacob (supplanter and deceiver) to Israel (prince of God). The entire event took place at Jabbok, which means "empty." [20] When Jacob was finally empty of self, God could then do his intimate work and proclaim destiny.

> *And Jacob was left alone; and there wrestled a man with him until the breaking of the day. And when he saw that he prevailed not against him, he touched the hollow of his thigh; and the hollow of Jacob's thigh was out of joint, as he wrestled with him. And he said, Let me go, for the day breaketh. And he said, I will not let thee go, except thou bless me. And he said unto him, What is thy name? And he said, Jacob. And he said, **Thy name shall be called no more Jacob, but Israel: for as a prince hast thou power with God and with men, and hast prevailed.** And Jacob asked him, and said, Tell me, I pray thee, thy name. And he said, Wherefore is it that thou dost ask after my name? And he blessed him there.*

Genesis 32:24-29 (emphasis mine)

Once again we notice the results of determination for destiny. Aaron and Hur had to remain determined to hold up Moses' arms. I am sure they grew just as weary as Moses, but they found their place in ministry and fulfilled their responsibility. Saints, as Aarons and Hurs we are being challenged to lay hold of our covenant promises, which will empower us to fulfill destiny.

Jacob held on until he received God's blessing. All too often we quit prematurely! Hanging on until you get the victory of becoming a new man is worth the fight; it is worth believing for and wrestling over. We must become like Jacob and declare to the Lord that we will NOT let go of Him until He blessed us! We too can become the blessed of the Lord if we devote ourselves to Him in every way.

We might need a good wrestling match with destiny to become more determined, but we can be certain that God desires to bless us. Fight for your promise and God will change your name!

How to receive a name change:

1) We must make a decision that it is time to change.
2) Realize that the enemy has lied and we have believed his lie concerning ourselves and others.
3) Repent for believing the lies and for receiving a false name from the enemy.
4) Begin to believe what God says about us.
5) We must become determined and know that receiving a new name from God is worth fighting for!
6) Don't let go until you get it!

Like Saul, it may take a road to Damascus experience before we experience a name change, but in the end it will be worth it! The name Saul means "desired,"[21] (implying what God has desired for us to be). Sometimes God may have to knock us off of our "high horse" (implying pride and arrogance) to change our names into Paul, which means "small or little,"[22] (implying humility). And in order for a Simon (one who hears)[23] to become a Peter (meaning a rock)[24] we may have to press into greater revelation to fully understand the benefits of a name change. Evidently, it is important because God had to change names for fulfillment of destiny.

However, in any case, the enemy who locked you into your prison does NOT want you to know and understand that God wants to change your name. Remember, the Amalekite stronghold is very seductive and the enemy will continually discourage you by speaking an old name over you. His plans are to deceive you into believing that you can never be changed or transformed into Christ's image.

Sickness and Disease

The enemy has planned assignments of sickness and disease! Since the name *Amalekite* means "desperately wicked" and "incurable sickness,"[25] the spirit will attempt to do exactly as his name states; continually attack us with his wickedness, sickness and disease. Satan has assigned spirits of wickedness to hold us captive in defiled, polluted behavior.

However, Dear Aarons and Hurs, we have the same empowerment available as Jacob. We can wrestle against the old sinful nature and hang onto the promise of the Spirit as God transitions each of us into a new name!

> *For we wrestle not against flesh and blood, but against principalities, against powers, against the rulers of the darkness of this world, against spiritual wickedness in high places.*

Eph 6:12

Keep in mind, the Amalekite stronghold is very sly in its tactics. First, we know that it lies in wait until we are tired and weary and, then, it mercilessly attacks. Secondly, we must always remember that this spirit promotes wickedness through temptations of lust, perversion, disobedience and the partaking of unclean things (through impure thoughts, impure actions or even areas of disobedience).

A *stronghold* is exactly what it says it is - a STRONG HOLD on us. What has "hold" of you? Is it pornography, lust, sexual perversion or is it fear, alcohol, or even drugs? A stronghold can be anything that holds us captive. I personally believe that a stronghold begins in the mind and in the thoughts. If we can begin to renew our minds with the Word of God, then we will initiate the tearing down of the fortress, which holds us captive.

By carefully examining Ephesians 6:12 once again, we notice that wickedness is seated in a "high place." Anytime something in our lives is seated in a higher position than Christ, it must be torn down. This could mean thoughts, belief systems, attitudes, lifestyles or any area where Christ does not rule and reign. In the Old Testament, the Lord sought after kings and leaders who would go up and tear down the altars in high places. God still seeks after men and women of God who will not allow satan to be enthroned in any area of their hearts and lives. We too must go up and tear down mindsets and false belief systems that have been exalted above the knowledge of God.

> *4) For the weapons of our warfare are not carnal, but mighty through God to the pulling down of strong holds;*
>
> *5) Casting down imaginations, and every high thing that exalteth itself against the knowledge of God, and bringing into captivity every thought to the obedience of Christ;*

2 Cor. 10: 4,5

The High Things

The high things in 2 Corinthians 10:4,5 are the things exalted above the character and Word of God, things such as thoughts, beliefs, and mindsets or ungodly lifestyle standards that are set higher than God's standards. We will not be able to fight against the Amalekite stronghold with carnal weapons, but rather we must fight with faith and the Word of the Lord. We must cast down our imaginations, meaning that we have to tear down old belief systems about ourselves and replace those thoughts with the Word of God. When the enemy attacks your mind and says that you will be barren and never experience the fullness of your promise, cast down that thought and replace it with a bold confession of faith. As a submitted believer...resist the devil and he must flee! (See James 4:7).

Spiritual wickedness is at its peak when the enemy can seduce us into believing his lies. Satan is a cruel taskmaster and he will attempt to bring much hardship upon God's children. Where wickedness is at work, satan's every evil purpose is being fulfilled.

The hospitals are filled with those afflicted with incurable diseases. The Amalekite spirit will captivate through disease, mental torment and mental illnesses. If satan can continue his attacks which cause us to remain weak and disabled, he will stalk us like a predator to completely devour us. However, if we have committed hearts, remain obedient, and pure in motive, it lessens the vulnerability for attack. By closing every door of sin, renewing the mind to the perfect will of God and remaining in obedience, the Lord can then become our stronghold and high tower. He desires to be our fortress and strength and He waits for our decisions to make Him Lord of our lives.

Through dedication to His purposes and repentance of past sins, the enemy can be defeated. <u>Where there is repentance, there is always a victory</u>. The enemy cannot overcome us unless we choose to surrender! So, stand firm and see God's promises to you fulfilled! Satan's goal is for you to concede and submit to his temptations of wickedness, but with God's authority you can rise above every circumstance and soar like an eagle.

If the enemy can entice the children of God to compromise and agree with his wickedness, he has gained legal entrance into their lives. With legal entrance, he can inflict heavy toil, great pain and incurable sickness upon leaders and those destined to be leaders. Satan is a master deceiver and he will use whatever tactics necessary to wear us out.

Don't Sell Your Birthright

The Amalekites were descendents of Esau. Remember Essau? He was the son of Jacob who sold his entire inheritance for a bowl of soup! Think of it, losing everything you have because of a fleshly desire. *Because Esau chose not to consider the value of his godly inheritance, God chose not to honor Esau.*

In fact, God was so upset about this that He declared himself as *God of Abraham, Isaac and JACOB…* not even mentioning being the God of Esau, who was originally the one to be named because of his birth priority! What does this speak today to each of us? We cannot under any condition or circumstance sell our birthright! No matter what fleshly desire attempts to seduce us, we must maintain our position of godly inheritance! Don't sell your birthright!

Esau's lack of self-discipline cancelled his spiritual destiny in God. This is also what happens to our destiny when we allow the flesh supremacy. If our flesh is in an exalted place of authority, we will forfeit the benefits of our inheritance. We will abort destiny if we "sell out" to the devil.

When the Amalekite spirit is in operation, our flesh is magnified. We become heavily tempted with worldly desires and we easily could sell out to the world. The enemy will come at our weakest moment and then seduce us to trade our purity and godliness for sinful worldly pleasures. We forfeit our leadership callings and spiritual passion, we forfeit our marriages and we forfeit destiny. Our birthright as children of God promises an inheritance. However, if we chose to be children of Belial, our inheritance is cancelled and there is no fulfillment of promise.

The Planting of the Lord

The Amalekites had a history of being a wandering tribe with no sense of permanence. As a result, there was no respect for covenant relationships neither among themselves nor with anyone else. Having no commitment to each other, they were self-indulgent and self-centered. They inherited from Esau the need for instant gratification and immediate satisfaction rather than the fruits of patience, long-suffering and peace.

Just as Esau disregarded the covenant he had with God, the same happened to many of his descendents. As a result of being a non-covenanted people, the descendents of Esau became enemies of God and continually battled against the Israelites generation after generation.

Because they were not a covenant people, they eventually became idol worshipers. As we've seen in previous chapters, the scripture speaks often concerning the curses upon generations of idol worship. When the Amalekite spirit is in operation, you will notice that many "things" come before God. Many are committed to sports, entertainment and pleasure rather than to God and His purposes. Very little time and attention are given to the House of God or to the Kingdom of God. There is little commitment to the future harvest when the Amalekite is in operation; all focus is on self and selfish gain and ambition. Church leaders become focused on building their own kingdoms rather than building THE KINGDOM.

Once again, remember where there is idolatry, there is sin and wickedness. Idolatry is prohibited by the Lord and considered an *accursed thing*. When idolatry is a stronghold, it is very difficult to get people to commit to servanthood because they are busy with other "things."

Everything becomes more important than serving in the House of the Lord or serving the cause of the Kingdom of God. However, without servants it is impossible for the necessary tasks to be completed in God's House. A handful of committed people cannot accomplish the work of needed hundreds.

When this ruthless spirit is working in the local church, there is a lack of commitment and church membership. Since the Amalekites were wanderers and were not committed, you will notice a wandering generation of believers moving from church to church, never committing and never joining as members. These wanderers will never become the plantings of the Lord.

God desires that we become planted so that we can bear fruit. Have you ever seen a fruit tree that is not planted bear any fruit? It is impossible for this to happen! Every tree must remain planted so that it can receive the nutrients from the soil. Without soil, nutrients, water and sunshine there is NO fruit tree that will prosper. How can we expect to bear fruit if we are never planted in one place long enough for our roots to take hold?

So often, as a pastor, I have witnessed those who are never able to stay in one place. There are many of God's children who are "conference addicted." They travel from one conference to the next, channel surf through television for "pick a pastor" programs, and never lock into any local assembly. They are un-accountable to anyone for their actions, but still consider themselves super-spiritual. Spiritual nomads are uncommitted and selfish toward serving in God's house. How sad that so many of God's saints are missing out on a tremendous blessing simply through the obedience of serving one another.

Division, Destruction and Death

Another strategy of the Amalekite stronghold is to create an atmosphere of disunity within the Body of Christ. If satan can bring disunity, then the enemy can destroy destiny and bring death to vision within a congregation.

The spirit first begins by speaking lies within a congregation. The accuser of the brethren works strongly in conjunction with the Amalekite spirit and begins to falsely accuse each member to one another. Soon strife dictates division; people become wounded, hurt and offended. Eventually, division occurs as the members begin to separate from one another. During the separation each member becomes vulnerable to attack. Since the Amalekites were well known for picking off the stragglers from a camp, we easily understand why this spirit tries to continually bring separation from a body of believers. As soon as a member withdraws from spiritual oversight and covering, the devil moves in immediately for the "hit".

Like a thief, the enemy's purpose is to steal the destiny of a corporate body as well as from an individual. Where churches are speaking truth and prophesying life and destiny, the enemy will continually attack that church body because the destroyer steals the seed. In Revelations 12:24 it says that the devourer stands at the time of birthing to steal the child. This is exactly what satan does today. He attacks the spiritual wombs of God's chosen with death assignments.

> *2) And she being with child cried, travailing in birth, and pained to be delivered.*
>
> *3) And there appeared another wonder in heaven; and behold a great red dragon, having seven heads and ten horns, and seven crowns upon his heads.*
>
> *4) And his tail drew the third part of the stars of heaven, and did cast them to the earth: and the dragon stood before the woman which was ready to be delivered, for to devour her child as soon as it was born.*

Rev 12:2-4

Within each of our spiritual wombs there are seeds of destiny that have been planted by God. As He has spoken His will, His word and His way over each of us, seeds have become impregnated within us, waiting for the appointed time to birth (destiny). The enemy will stand close guard, just waiting for an opportunity to destroy our destiny. Our destiny involves every promise the Lord has given us. Every prophetic word, every anointed proclamation we have heard from God involves our destiny and purpose on this earth. <u>The enemy knows that if he can steal the seed, steal our hope and steal our promise, then he has won the battle.</u>

Satan lies in wait to separate, isolate, deceive and then seduce us into areas of sin and apostasy! Be on guard!

If we know his tactics, we can thwart his predetermined victory. We can quickly retaliate against his planned attacks by confessing our promises, staying in the Word of God and meeting corporately with believers. We also must be committed to travail with every promise until we fully birth God's plan for our lives. Just as a woman in labor must commit to the full process for the destiny of her child, we also must commit to the process until we experience results!

In the midst of warfare concerning our destiny, we are to be like the King of Israel who was to strike the arrows against the ground to <u>utterly destroy all</u> of the enemy's plans. We must not settle for less than what God has planned for us. The King of Israel smote the arrows only a few times, representing a limited victory. We are to learn from this example and be determined to smite our arrows until all of the enemies' plans are destroyed! Smite your arrows against your ground of promise to insure your destiny today! (See 2 Kings 13:18-19)

It is time for you, the Aarons and Hurs, to <u>strike</u> the enemy and make a bold confession:

1. against any physical infirmity or weakness, helplessness and loss of vision.
2. against compromise, lack of self-discipline and indulgence of the flesh.
3. against becoming a spiritual nomad and not being firmly planted.
4. against remaining in darkness, where the Amalekite attacks.
5. against selling your birthright and compromising your call in God.

<u>List below other areas to strike your arrows against.</u>

Chapter Seven

GOD'S RODS OF RIGHTEOUSNESS

*I*t was Easter Sunday. What a glorious spring morning. The sun was shining, the flowers were blooming; signs of life were budding forth. *Such a glorious representation of a new day, this Easter Sunday, I said to myself as we drove to church.*

My thoughts were racing as I focused on the Sunday church service. Oh Lord, please build Your Church! You died that we might live. Your blood has insured victory on every side. This is resurrection Sunday. Lord, resurrect every area in your Church that appears dead.

It had been a LONG dry season. I was desperate for God to move upon our behalf. I needed to experience a fresh touch of His power. Weary and experiencing hope deferred, our leaders needed a touch from His hand. Just as the Scripture had prophesied, ...hope deferred makes the heart sick...(Proverbs 13:12) we were experiencing the adversity of hopelessness.

The Scripture concerning God building His Church began to rush through my mind.

And I say also unto thee, That thou art Peter, and upon this rock I will build my church; and the gates of hell shall not prevail against it.

Matthew 16:18

I began to meditate on every aspect of the scripture; God said the gates of hell would never prevail against His church...why then did it seem as if hell was victorious over our situations?

Lord, I want to be like Peter, I desire to become that ROCK upon which you can build. Equip me to become stable in every way so that I am a part of building your church! I cried out silently in prayer.

It was then that I heard the Lord speak clearly the words that changed my mindsets on building His Church. First of all, the Lord began to minister to me that HE would build HIS Church.

The Church was HIS and not mine. Though I co-pastored the congregation, it was still HIS. My part was to co-labor WITH Him, but even as I did my part, fulfilling my destiny, it was still HIS Church! It was time to R-E-L-E-A-S-E it to Him.

Secondly, the Lord began to minister concerning the spiritual warfare of the Church. For years, I pictured the Church as a fortress, standing firm and fortified, but in a <u>defensive</u> position; simply defending its boundaries. I envisioned satan and his demonic forces attacking the church, aggressively moving forward in an offensive position attempting to destroy the Church. However, the Lord spoke to me that the Church was NOT simply standing still, but rather that the Church WAS <u>MOVING</u> forth in an offensive position. The Church was moving toward the goal of victory, and hell was NOT going to be able to rise up against the constant force of power from God's Church!

I had been on the defense too long! I had developed a defensive mentality, almost <u>expecting</u> to be falsely accused and blamed for other people's problems! But, God reassured me that He was the one in charge of the Church and HE would build it. The Church of God is NOT on the defense, but actively, aggressively pursuing its enemy!

And thirdly, the Lord said that the Church would need new "rods of authority" in the days ahead. He began to minister to me concerning Moses' famed rod of supernatural influence. Moses would stretch forth his rod, given to him by God, and miracles would occur. The Lord revealed that His **believers** of today were becoming **rods** in His hand, and that we were His battle-axe and His weapons of righteousness. He went on to say that the **righteousness** that His leaders walk in would defeat the enemy because righteousness is a weapon, which defeats the enemy!

Neither yield ye your members as instruments of unrighteousness unto sin: but yield yourselves unto God, as those that are alive from the dead, and your members as instruments of righteousness unto God.

Romans 6:13

Thou art my battle axe and weapons of war: *for with thee will I break in pieces the nations, and with thee will I destroy kingdoms;*

Jer.51:20 (emphasis mine)

God's Rods...Aaron and Hur!

I then realized that if the enemy could seduce the Aaron's and Hurs into sin and areas of defilement that he could continue to steal life from God's Church. After all, just like Moses, every minister needs an Aaron and Hur. Moses was very blessed to have two strongly committed leaders to hold up his arms and a Joshua to lead the troops in battle. Alongside every Joshua, a Caleb needs to rise up and become part of the army.

I began to understand the scheme of the Amalekite stronghold that came to constantly discourage me by the following progression:

seducing the sheep into sin that destroyed their destiny
when their destiny was destroyed it effected CORPORATE destiny
leaving very few committed leaders to hold up our arms
removing generals to lead the battles in spiritual warfare
stealing the "rods" of authority promised to us by the Lord
stealing vision and causing hope deferred

I knew that it had become my season to understand the significance of these new rods of authority. This rod was not only righteousness, but it was a "people" who were righteous for they were the rods! Being a righteous people made them a rod of God's authority on the earth! The Lord wants to hold us up as a rod before our enemy. He will say, "satan, do you see my sheep? They are my rods of authority because they are righteous. Therefore, satan, you must flee as they stand as rods of my authority before you!

Isn't that an awesome thought? Imagine your church congregation coming to a Red Sea experience. God holds up your pastor and leaders as rods of righteousness before that Red Sea and a miracle occurs! Satan's plans of destruction are defeated because of righteous leadership.

Let's take this thought another step. What about YOU and YOUR Red Sea? God will do the very same for your situations. He will use YOU as a rod against every Red Sea and you can cross over onto dry land. We are ALL called to be rods of righteousness and the Lord desires that we ALL experience victory on every side!

The enemy will especially attack those who are destined to become the Aarons and Hurs to a Moses. The appointed and chosen supporters to every leader will be weapons (rods) in the purposes of God. Moses had his rod that he stretched across the Red Sea, a rod that brought forth water from a rock, but he also had rods of righteousness that held up his arms. The Lord revealed that He desired to do the same for every senior leader and every Moses that He had called to minister! Begin to believe now for the strength to become a rod of righteousness. God desires for many of you to become an Aaron and Hur to your spiritual Moses. If you are a Moses, in any spiritual capacity, God will use you as a rod to part Red Seas, strike rocks and hard places for water, as well as raise up many Aarons and Hurs.

Rephidim: The Places of Support

In Exodus 17:8, we read where Moses was leading the Israelites in the wilderness. Not only had he previously used his rod at the Red Sea, but also now had drawn water from a rock at the commandment of the Lord. After the people were refreshed, they immediately went into battle against Amalek, the king of the Amalekites. Moses instructed Joshua to choose men to fight against

Amalek, knowing that the next day Moses, himself, would view the battle from the top of the hill. Moses was to stand with an outstretched rod, once again, to insure another victory.

> *17) Then came Amalek, and fought with Israel in Rephidim.*
> *18) And Moses said unto Joshua, Choose us out men, and go out, fight with Amalek: to morrow I will stand on the top of the hill with the rod of God in mine hand.*

Ex 17:8-9

Moses understood the importance of remaining in a position where people could see him stretch out his rod. It is the same in the Church today. A congregation NEEDS to see a Moses holding up his rod. The congregation NEEDS to witness leaders walking in righteousness. Also, they NEED to see Aarons and Hurs who are committed to holding up the arms of Moses. If a congregation does not witness a rod constantly held high, the sheep will begin to scatter! The Amalekite spirit is committed to destroying the Aarons and Hurs in order to split a congregation.

Moses had faith that God would move each time he would stretch out his rod. Time and time again, Moses had used his rod as a device to challenge Pharaoh. He would stretch out the rod, use his faith by God's command, and miracles would occur. A Red Sea parted, water spouted forth from a silent rock, becoming a symbol of stability, breakthrough, and a multitude of wonders. Now, as part of the battle strategy, Moses would hold up the same rod and release another victory, this time against the Amalekites.. Moses would take a firm stand and hold out the rod to encourage Israel...it was to be a sure sign of victory.

Maybe Moses did not take into account the length of the battle when he volunteered to extend the rod...and keep it there! (How long did Moses actually have to hold up the rod for all of Israel to cross over the Red Sea, anyway?!) Or, maybe Moses knew that God would make a way, as He had done so many times before, to continue to support the rod. At any rate, Moses did not retreat from his original declaration; being fully determined to keep the rod extended for all of Israel to see.

Moses did eventually grow tired during the battle and his arm muscles waxed weary. Can't you picture it? Moses is desperately attempting to hold up the rod, his muscles beginning to flinch, possibly spasm, tempting him to let down the rod? Moses is thinking....*SPASM, Spasm! Hey, guys, can't you see? SPASM*!

In verse 10, Joshua is leading the Israelites into battle while Hur and Aaron stand with Moses at the top of the hill named Rephidim. The scripture says that as long as Moses help up his hand (holding the rod) **Israel prevailed** against Amalek. BUT, when Moses let down his hand, then **Amalek prevailed**!

Use your imagination again and picture yourself watching the scene where Moses is holding up his hand. Israel sees Moses holding his rod. A roar rips through their spirits as they rise up with tremendous vigor and faith in God. They smote the Amalekites on the left and on the right!

Moses then becomes weary; his hand begins to falter. The rod is no longer in sight! Fear grips the hearts of the Israelites. "Where is Moses? Where is the favor of God?" The soldiers begin to waver; their faith weakens while they struggle to see the rod of victory.

The Amalekites are also watching for the rod. They notice Moses' hand fall to his side, the rod is NOWHERE in sight!

"NOW!" The Amalekite general gives the charge! "Now! Go! The battle is ours!" The Amalekites begin to slay the Israelites; the tide has turned as the Israelites lose sight of the rod.

Aaron and Hur rush to Moses to grab his arms and up goes the rod of authority!

The Israelites can see it once again! "The Lord is with us! No weapon formed against us will prosper!"

Finally, a victory occurs. Israel has won as the result of awesome teamwork; Moses with Aaron and Hur and a Joshua commanding the troops! No victory is substantial without teamwork. We need each other. An effective army learns to fight together and remain together.

What is the message I am trying convey? The significance is that the Amalekite stronghold will attempt to win many battles by removing the Aarons and Hurs. The Amalekites were at the battle, observing what happened when Aaron and Hur held up Moses' hands. Eventually, they caught onto the battle plan. In fact, if they could have shot arrows to destroy Aaron and Hur, they probably would have! They would have aimed at Moses also, I'm sure. In any case, satan knows that he can weaken every leader if there is no one to hold up their arms.

Verse 12 says that Aaron and Hur took a stone and placed it under Moses for him to sit, and they held up his hands; one on one side and the other on the other side. They committed to do this until the end of the day. Because of the servanthood of these two devoted men, Israel gained a victory over Amalek.

It is interesting to note that this battle was in the area of *Rephidim*, which means, "to support" (as holding up from the bottom).[26] If every saint in the kingdom of God fully understood the principles of servanthood, there would be continual victory in the House of God. However, because the Amalekite spirit deceives God's children into believing that their positions of servanthood are unimportant and menial, it is difficult to keep servants motivated.

While we pastored a local church, I observed too often how the enemy would constantly attack our Aarons and Hurs. Our pastoral team and our team of leaders were chosen by God to support us and hold up our arms. We would not have been able to press on into our destiny if it were not due to the commitment of those who supported us in our local assembly. I have thanked the Lord over and over for so many of our precious leaders and saints who committed to support us and stand with us; especially in times of great adversity.

Dear ones, if you are an Aaron and a Hur to your leaders, God bless you! The work of the Lord could not be possible without your commitment and dedication to the plans and purposes of God.

The Thief Robs the House of Servants

Robbing God's House of needed servants is satan's strategy. Just as we read of Moses and his devoted servants, if leaders do not have help…there will be no victory. We are all part of God's army, and we each have a part to play; destiny to fulfill. One person may be called to be a general, another a private. One may be a senior leader, another prayer warrior. But not a single one is more important to God than the other! It is a matter of delegated authority, and God is the Commander and Chief! Aaron and Hur were just as important as Moses in the battle against Amalek. Their unified effort guaranteed the victory for all of Israel.

Caleb, the victor who got his mountain was referred to as a SERVANT (see Numbers 14:24). Though he had a different spirit, he was, more importantly, a servant of the Lord. A servant is one who simply serves. Not concerned about title or position, but rather serving the Lord's purpose. Aaron and Hur were serving Moses, but more importantly they were serving the cause of God's full plan of destiny for Israel. Saints, this battle was bigger than Moses, bigger than Joshua, and bigger than Aaron and Hur. The plan is all about HIM. It is the same in today's battle. It is not about US and receiving our victories…it is about HIM and establishing His Kingdom on earth.

The Devil Does Not Play Fair!

Satan is underhanded and deceitful. He is unethical and ruthless in his tactics against us. His strategy is to bring disharmony, stirring strife among God's army. Fighting among ourselves is sure defeat, and the devil knows it. A battle inside the camp is the most deadly wound. As a senior pastor I have observed his tactics for years. I have observed how he causes strife and discontentment among the watchmen on the walls. The devil will attempt to contaminate the intercessors with malicious gossip and slander. Prayer warriors who are called to guard the walls of the church are often seduced into power struggles, rebellion and strife; creating a very infectious wound. Contamination spreads onto others as they begin to make phone calls with false accusations, not only to each other as intercessors but to others in the body. You may have heard this contaminated voice….it sounds similar to this:

> While in prayer, the Lord showed me that there was sin in the camp. Is God saying the same to you? I can't worship there anymore!
> While I was interceding I heard the Lord say that I was supposed to leave the church. I know that there are others that are to leave also. Did you hear the same from God? Will you help me alert others that it is time to leave?
> Did you know that while in prayer I heard the Lord say that He was removing His Spirit from the church?

> While in prayer, I saw the name "Ichabod" written across the altar of the church. I know I can hear from God. We need to alert the other intercessors! Will you help me make the calls and warn others?

This voice at times may sound totally innocent, but the motive is very impure. The hidden agenda behind this "concerned intercessor" is to lead others away from godly protection and oversight and unto herself/himself. Many church splits are a result of intercessory teams feeling that they are the ones called to "lead" the church with what THEY see in the Spirit realm. When, in fact, they are to remain pure in their hearts, pray for the leaders and support them with their prayers.

At the defeat of Ai the Lord did not go to the intercessors to have them discern the stronghold. God spoke to Joshua and Joshua only and had Joshua deal with the sin in the camp. Intercessors will discern sin and they are to pray, very discreetly, concerning sin. However, they are not called to judge the sin; that is the Lord's responsibility. God places leaders in position through His delegated authority and it is not the intercessors' responsibly to lead the sheep.

Since it is satan's strategy to disassemble authority within the local assemblies, he will most likely target all of the support systems. This includes all areas of leadership (pastors, elders, deacons, department heads) as well as servants and intercessors. I believe that we are ALL called to serve in God's house in one capacity of another. If you are not in leadership now, you are most likely destined to be one at some level. If you serve at any capacity, the devil will try and destroy you. Satan does not want you to fulfill your destiny and he will use whatever tactic he can to deceive, seduce and separate you from God's plan.

Purity Begins with God's Leaders

I have heard my spiritual father, Bishop Bill Hamon, preach on this subject many times. I have heard him often say that if we do not deal with our sin in private, God will begin to shout it from the rooftops. This is frightening, and yet it is happening more and more. We can all remember times when there was television exposure concerning certain Christian leaders. If some had repented and turned from sin, there would not have been such tremendous, worldwide knowledge and exposure of their sin. I believe these times of exposures may have been necessary for the leaders to recognize the fact that God is calling for purity among his leaders. God is sovereignly building His church. He is laying the axe to every root against His will and calling each of us to purity and holiness. He is setting a standard of purity before us and molding us into the image of Christ and He is beginning with His LEADERS!

Righteousness will become a rod of authority that we will use to defeat our enemy in these last days. We must learn to fight under the right banner in the right season. At this time, in order to defeat the defilement of the Amalekite stronghold we must gather under the correct standard.

Coming under banners of religion will not insure a victory; however gathering beneath the banner of God's plans and purposes will always release victory. The Church must recognize her times and seasons. There is a time to fight under the banner of faith, or beneath His banner of prophecy, but at all times and in every season we need to recognize WHICH banner we are to gather under and fight with! Knowing this and acting with faith upon it will release a rod of authority released for a great victory.

Servants, Rise Up!

It is time to rise up and possess the gate of your enemies! Gates represent open attacks from satan. A gate is every area in your life that is open and vulnerable to attack. We are experiencing wake up calls; God is exposing every area of sin. He is searching the hearts of His leaders and laying His axe to the root of every tree that is not bearing fruit. If the devil can keep us in bondage to sin, he will continue to win the battle. He will cause us to doubt God's Word, doubt our destiny, stir strife and discontentment and keep us in unforgiveness. He will study every weakness and then move with intents of captivity. Leaders must realize that it is our appointed time to rise up, put the enemy beneath our feet, repent and turn from all areas of wickedness. Remember, we cannot be held captive in darkness for we are children of the LIGHT! However, by tolerating darkness through sin, we leave ourselves open for attack. If we remain disobedient and not *utterly destroy all*, we may become like King Saul and seduced into apostasy.

We can now begin, with God's help, to take our personal gates. By taking this promised spiritual ground, we will experience personal breakthroughs which will lead to corporate breakthroughs. The revolving doors that have been legal entrances into our lives will be permanently destroyed, as we become effective leaders in God's army!

Are you called to be a leader in the House of God? Have you allowed the enemy to deceive you into leaving your post? If so, it's time to get back into the battle! You must realign with your destiny links. Know where you are to be planted and remain there. Hold up the arms of your leaders and fight the good fight of faith.

For those of you who have left your post, repentance will empower you to move forward into destiny. Ask the Lord to forgive you for leaving your assigned position and then recommit your life to His perfect will and destiny for your life.

To insure that you walk in continuous victory, it is important to make note of situations, which caused you to leave your post in the first place. Was it disappointment in leaders? Did someone wound you and as a result you isolated yourself from the Body? Did you go through a divorce? Are you suffering with a stronghold of shame? Be determined to never allow anything to rob your destiny. List below the reasons your destiny may be hindered.

1.

2.

3.

4.

5.

Write below the ways that you plan to change your situation and get back into the battle.

Make this bold confession right now.

I Will Take My Mountain and Achieve My Destiny!

Chapter Eight

TOUCHING GOD'S ANOINTED

...Touch not mine anointed, and do my prophets no harm.

1 Chronicles 16:22

The devil is determined to *touch* the anointed ones of God. The word *touch* in this passage of scripture means, "to touch, reach, **strike**, defeat and be **struck by disease**." The Amalekite spirit, is pilfering God's anointed. The devil, working through the Amalekite stronghold, is weakening God's saints, little by little, strategy by strategy, slowly but steadily stealing our strength and anointing. Satan intends to strike against us with methods of wickedness and if possible inflict all types of sickness and disease.

Just as the Amalekite spirit struck against and seduced Saul, he seduces anointed believers today. Saul was struck with the seduction of disobedience and pride. Seduction is not limited to sexual perversion, nor limited to disobedience and pride. Please remember this; seduction also involves being seduced into believing a lie. If one of the enemy's strategies is to strike with sickness and disease, then know that his plan is to seduce us into <u>believing the lie that we cannot be healed</u>. Or, that God's will is for us to remain sick! There are many scriptures, which declare that it is God's divine will to heal us. God, Himself, declares that He is our healer! (see Exodus 15:26.)

Saul was only one of those who had destiny stolen. The Amalekite stronghold negatively influenced him in many different ways. <u>Let's review and once again observe the different methods of destruction used against King Saul and how the Amalekite stronghold targets us today:</u>

Method # 1: Disobedience

Saul was deceived into disobedience. As he led the attack against the Amalekites he chose NOT to utterly destroy all as God had told him. He feared man more than God.

The Lord is requiring obedience from today's leaders. We can no longer fear man, nor remain in religious tradition. We must also realize that when we embrace more of His Spirit there is a requirement to let go of the old. Old behavior, old thought patterns and the traditions of man must be sanctified and tried with His holy fire.   The Amalekite stronghold, if allowed, will convince you that you do not have to change to move forward with His Spirit. Just as the devil convinced Saul that he did not have to "utterly destroy all," he will convince us of the same…if we are not alert! You will desire to hold onto previous patterns of sin and sin behavior. Just as the Israelites wanted to return to the leeks and garlic of Egypt, you will be tempted to go back into defilement.

Method #2: Rebellion

Saul rebelled against the instructions of God; meaning that he chose to do opposite of what God said. Rebellion is not only disobedience, but it is opposition and defiance to one who is in authority.

When a leader is disobedient and in rebellion, their offspring of spiritual reproduction will eventually be the same. A leader who has fruits of rebellion will have a congregation in rebellion. This is a spiritual principle of sowing and reaping. Saul chose to defy God's commandments and therefore the Prophet Samuel brought correction. In the Word of the Lord brought by the prophet,

God proclaimed his displeasure of the King and removed the kingdom from Saul.

Method #3: Lack of Repentance

Saul did not repent for his disobedience, for true repentance brings change. Instead, bitterness and resentment built within Saul's heart. He did not take personal responsibility for his choices of disobedience, but rather began to blame others. He blamed "the people" for his sin:

> *And Samuel said, Hath the LORD as great delight in burnt offerings and sacrifices, as in obeying the voice of the LORD? Behold, to obey is better than sacrifice, and to hearken than the fat of rams. For rebellion is as the sin of witchcraft, and stubbornness is as iniquity and idolatry. Because thou hast rejected the word of the LORD, he hath also rejected thee from being king.*
> *And Saul said unto Samuel, I have sinned: for I have transgressed the commandment of the LORD, and thy words: because I feared the people, and obeyed their voice.*

1 Samuel 15:22-24

Today, there is much revelation concerning repentance. In fact, repentance has become a major move of God's Spirit. Strategic prayer revivals are held in convention centers where national prayer leaders call for corporate repentance. Prayer warriors are repenting for city and national governments, leaders are repenting for the sins against the Native Americans and other minorities. This has brought healing to the nations.

An Amalekite stronghold fights against repentance. Instead the spirit reinforces shame and blame; which will become a cycle that hinders us from taking responsibility for our own actions.   There is also a reinforcement of co-dependency (needing approval of others) and control issues. Remember, Saul blamed others for his actions, wanted the people's approval and took matters into his own hands (control).

Saints must always remain teachable and accountable. They should also strive to mature to levels of trusting God and His ability to build His church. If there are control issues, they need to be recognized, repented of and then laid at the cross. This is the only way we can fully embrace the NEW place God has for each of us.

Method #4: The Effects of Witchcraft

Once again, it is necessary to discuss witchcraft from a different perspective. Witchcraft is often misunderstood in many churches. All too often we are reminded of the *Wicked Witch of the West* in *The Wizard of Oz*. It is not an old ugly woman with a crooked nose and warts dressed in black with a pointed hat riding upon a broom. **<u>Witchcraft is a demonic system that gains power through rebellion and stubbornness of God's people.</u>** Notice that in the previous passage (1 Samuel 15:22-24) it states that *...rebellion is as the sin of witchcraft....*

Where there are rebellious hearts there is witchcraft. Witchcraft is a form of divination. One method of divination used against the Church is in the form of <u>false prophecy</u>. Though the scripture speaks of false prophets who give false prophecies, this is not what I am referring to at this time. Many times false prophecy is the enemy falsely prophesying to the children of God. Very often, without realizing it, we open the door to this stronghold when we are in rebellion. Defying God's authority gives the devil an open gate to speak lies into our ears. Again, before we comprehend our action, this lying spirit seduces us and then the sin becomes our master.

The Apostle Paul names witchcraft *sorcery* as one of the works of the flesh (Gal 5:20). We know that witchcraft has its origin through carnality and then succumbs to forms of witchcraft through control, manipulation, stubbornness and rebellion. Control and manipulation are areas that most of us contend with, yet is another form of witchcraft. The Church is not exempt to the spirits operating in control. Many people in congregations control and manipulate to get their way. People with large amounts of money use their finances as tools to force action of their opinions.. Others control leadership with threats and intimidation. The Amalekite stronghold is simply another spirit that promotes manipulation and control tactics.

Most of us are aware that witchcraft involves the occult. Saul opened the door to the occult when he became disobedient and rebellious. After his defiance of God's orders, the scripture states that an evil spirit was allowed to come upon Saul and torment him. (see 1 Samuel 16:23) Years later, Saul had demeaned himself to the point that he sought out the witch at Endor, which later led to his ultimate destruction and death.

Caught in the act of disobedience and rebellion, true repentance would have replaced God's favor back upon Saul's life. Scripture does point out that Saul admitted his sin, but never repented and changed.

Knowing the outcome of Saul's disobedience and rebellion should challenge each of us to guard our hearts and actions. When we give of our tithes and offerings, we must give with joy and pure hearts. Any attempt to control ministries or ministers with money will only grieve God and possibly open doors of witchcraft. Once again, being quick to repent will always bring us nearer to the heart of the Father.

Method #5: The Fear of Man

In 1 Samuel 13:11, Saul is once again blaming the people for his sins of disobedience. He was to wait for the Prophet Samuel to make the sacrifice unto the Lord. Instead of waiting as instructed, Saul performed the sacrifice prematurely. Saul stated that he did so because he "...saw that the people were scattering from me...and that the Philistines were assembling." In other words he was afraid that if he did not go ahead and perform the sacrifice, even though God said not to, that the people would leave him.

This is what is referred to as the fear of man.

People in godly authority are often tempted in the same manner. Pressures come from people who desire their own way. Many saints use intimidation and control to get what they desire. They will throw around their power; use their influence to take people out of a church. If leadership succumbs to people-pleasing measures rather than standing in their godly authority and doing what is correct, it opens the doors to controlling powers of witchcraft within the church. Satan will often attempt to move forth in illegitimate authority and cause strife within a congregation.

Saul was more concerned with pleasing people than pleasing the Lord. He had a defiled root system in his life; a root system full of selfishness and self-centeredness that would not submit to the instructions of the Lord. The Word of God says that the fear of man will bring a snare upon us. This snare will be our destruction due to disobedience. It is more important to be obedient to the Lord than to operate in the fear of man.

Leaders must always be more concerned with pleasing God rather than pleasing man. This does not mean, however, that leaders are to be unaccountable. In fact, it strongly implies that there is an even greater accountability that occurs in the hearts of leaders when they DO follow God and not man! Remaining open to correction and continuing to be teachable only increases with increased leadership responsibility.

Method #6: Loss of Vision

When Saul was first chosen as king, he was fearful. He actually ran from the call. The Prophet Samuel anointed him as king, though Saul did not desire the call. When he finally surrendered to be king, God was faithful to pour his favor upon him. Life seemed good for Saul UNTIL he fought the Amalekites. Suddenly the Amalekite spirit struck out against the leader and he was seduced into apostasy. The favored king was rebellious and disregarded the Word of the Lord.

Is it like that with us at times? We go through life wanting to be used of the Lord, knowing that we have a destiny? Then God calls us and suddenly we feel inadequate and try to RUN? Then we FINALLY submit to the call and we go into battle against the enemy of our soul. SUDDENLY we are faced with an Amalekite spirit who seduces us into sin and we are BACK where we started?

Sometimes do you feel as I - one step forward, two steps back?

There is an Amalekite attempting to steal your destiny! Don't stop now, repent and start again!

Saul had lost his vision in the attempt to take the Amalekites. He knew what he was instructed to do. He could most likely taste the victory; see the dedicated spoils given to the Lord, yet he was seduced into rebellion and disobedience. No longer could he see the prize of obedience. No longer was obedience enough....fame, fortune, individual selfish victory overrode his godly vision.

The scripture says that when there is no vision, the people perish. (Proverbs 29:18). When Saul lost vision he began to die. Death was pronounced over his kingship, death came upon him and he became tormented and anguished for the rest of his life.

Within each of us is a God-given vision. That vision is what I refer to as destiny. When destiny is stolen, vision is stolen. When we lose vision we often feel as if we are dead. However, if we will repent then the Lord will be faithful to resurrect what seemed to be dead.

Many times I have felt that I have lost vision. Especially when I am going through an extreme demonic attack, I want to quit and throw in the towel! So many times I have been tempted to run away from my calling. I often have "wishions" where I am suffering for Jesus in Hawaii or some far away tropic island in paradise. ("Wishions" are our wishes that we mistake for true visions from God.) Of course my pastoring responsibility would be to the harvest of tropical flowers and the fish in the OCEAN! My "wishion" involves a life on EASY STREET (is there one?). There have been numerous times that I have lost hope and it seemed as if NOTHING God said was coming to pass. It was in many of those seasons that the Lord told me that it was DEATH TO SEASON and NOT DEATH TO VISION. Many times the enemy will twist things and convince you that you have missed it! You will feel dry and desolate. But hang on! It may be simply a death to the season and not time for the vision to come to pass. God is not a liar, what He has promised He will surely do! Hang in there and Fight for your promise!

It's time to repent.

Take a few moments and repent of:

Control	Agreeing with satan's lies
Manipulation	Lack of submission
Pride	Illegitimate authority
Rebellion	The fear of man
Disobedience	

Ask the Lord to renew your vision and empower you to fulfill destiny.

Chapter Nine

A Time Such as This

...thou art come into the kingdom for such a time as this

Esther 4:14

ust as Queen Esther came forth at her appointed time, it is an appointed time for the Body of Christ. It is our anointed and appointed season to arise and come to the forefront, moving purposefully into designated places of spiritual authority. Esther, however, did not suddenly arrive at destiny. She, as most of us can also testify, endured much preparation and later opposition as she pursued destiny.

Esther, in preparation for marriage, was anointed with specific perfumes. It was customary to cleanse, purify and anoint the female body in preparation for the king. In like matter, the Body of Christ is being cleansed to insure a sweet fragrance that the Lord seeks. The deep cleansing and purification is preparation and prelude to her intimate intercession and relationship with the Husband-man.

As previously discussed, for twelve months Esther was bathed in exotic and expensive oils. The number twelve is symbolic of new government and authority meaning that this purification process was necessary as she moved in her destined authority. Esther's destiny was to shift her government! She was chosen by God to change decrees of death against her own people. Many of us go through similar procedures of the process before we are released and empowered to rule and reign in spiritual authority. We also are purified and deeply cleansed to prepare us for purpose and destiny. We are individually cleansed from all unrighteousness, iniquity and impurity, which better prepares us for the high calling of Christ Jesus. Just as Esther, we are called to shift governmental decrees, bring a shift to our families, neighborhoods, nations and areas of business! Today, as we study the story of Esther, we notice that she symbolized the Body of Christ fulfilling destiny...*one step at a time.*

Step after step after step toward destiny Esther was prepared, purified, and cleansed as the future bride patiently awaited her specific position of authority. We can easily identify with Esther's process of preparation. Day after day after day we endure God's process, waiting for our specific times of breakthrough and times of fulfillment.

The Plot of Haman, the Amalekite

Many theologians have questioned the importance of the book of Esther. Though God is not mentioned throughout the entire book, one can clearly see that the book reveals God's planned strategy to save His chosen people. I am convinced that the book is not only divinely inspired, but also that specific warfare strategy is revealed against the "destiny thief," the Amalekite spirit.

When Esther was chosen as queen, an immediate opposition occurred against her and her people. The Amalekite stronghold arose once again to destroy another leader's destiny. This time the spirit worked through the individual, Haman. Haman, who was a favored prince of King Ahusuerus was placed in an authoritative position over all the Jews. All the people, save Mordecai (Esther's cousin) bowed down in homage to Haman as he paraded through the city streets. Haman, feeling humiliated and angered from Mordecai's lack of demanded respect, became enraged, and immediately devised a scheme to destroy Mordecai and ALL the Jews. It is not unlikely that satan used Haman as his pawn to abort the destiny of Israel, for Haman was a descendent of Agag...an Amalekite! (Esther 3:1)

Once again, this destiny thief spins its web of wickedness aimed at chosen leaders and all of God's chosen people! The devil recognizes that if he can re-move God's chosen from destined authority...the victory is his. This is why satan targets those in leadership positions. Any military officer is aware that if you are able to remove the head, the body dies!   Thinking in the natural, when the head is sick, the entire body suffers. Have you ever experienced a migraine headache? You cannot think, function, or make quality decisions if the head hurts. If satan can attack the head, the body cannot fully function.

Haman approached the king of Persia with his demonically inspired idea that all Jews needed to be destroyed. He convinced the king to believe that the Jews were rebellious toward the king's authority, that they were dangerous and that if they were not destroyed they would hinder kingly progress. Haman's webs of deceit were laced with manipulative words convincing the king that the Jews did not respect nor support the king's authority and if not destroyed the king's position would be jeopardized. Haman was full of wrath because Morde-cai did not show him reverence and bow down to him; therefore a plot of re-venge was hatched from this demonically controlled individual. Haman's pride fueled his fury to destroy God's anointed.

> *And when Haman saw that Mordecai bowed not, nor did him rev-erence, then was Haman full of wrath. 6 And he thought scorn to lay hands on Mordecai alone; for they had shewed him the people of Mordecai: wherefore Haman sought to destroy all the Jews that were throughout the whole kingdom of Ahasuerus, even the people of Mordecai.*

Esther 3:5-6

The same plot of destruction is assigned to us if we refuse to *bow down* to the enemy's strategy. Once we take a stand, as Mordecai, the Amalekite is swift to devise a strategy of destruction. But hold on....you, as a modern-day Esther has been prepared for such a time as this! You are coming forth in your due season to destroy the wickedness of the Amalekite.

After Haman convinced King Ahasuerus that the Jews were rebelling against his crown, he issued a decree to terminate all living Jews; not understanding that Queen Esther would also be destroyed. Quite clearly the king was influenced by the wicked Amalekite spirit to destroy the destiny of God's chosen and anointed. Haman was so determined to destroy the Jews he actually offered to finance the entire extermination! Basically, he was planning to plunder his enemies and take the spoils. Doesn't that exhibit the same tactics of the Amalekites in earlier history?

Remember, the Amalekites would attack the weak and feeble and take the spoils? It had been 500 years since Israel's first encounter with the Amalekites (following Israel's release from Egypt; Ex. 17:8-16), and the war was continued as prophesied. The Lord had proclaimed (see Exodus 17:16) that Israel would *continually* be at war with the Amalekites because they did NOT **utterly destroy all!**

*For he said, Because the LORD hath sworn that the LORD will have war with Amalek **from generation to generation.***

Ex 17:16

Now, half a century later, satan's seed planted years ago through Amalek is resurrected in another generation. Satan has never been quick to "throw in the towel" and quit. He continues to seek out our weak areas until he finds a gate of entrance. In Haman's case, satan had an open door to use him because of his pride and arrogance. Haman desired power and recognition and when satan can find someone similar to Haman to work through, he will move in quickly to hinder and destroy God's anointed. Saints, it is time to take a firm stand against this stronghold so that our generations can experience their godly destiny.

When I think of Haman I am reminded of Adolph Hitler who also attempted to annihilate the entire Jewish race. Over six million of God's chosen people were ruthlessly and inhumanely murdered. Could it be that the same Amalekite stronghold also influenced Hilter? Hitler was definitely deceived by demonic spirits and manifested pride and arrogance; very similar to Haman's actions. Hitler thrived on power, prestige and authority and destroyed everyone who exemplified insubordination. He demanded that people *bow down* and pay him homage in every situation.

Esther was called forth at an appointed time to intercede for God's people. She had been prepared, chosen and now was her anointed time of intercession. Her cousin, Mordecai, exposed the plans of destruction and she, as the queen, approached the king with God-given favor. Esther called a fast and approached the king on behalf of herself and the Jews. Esther laid down her life for the destiny of her people. Because her heart was pure and she walked in God's favor the king heard her pleas for safety. Esther's sacrificial attempt saved an entire nation. The Amalekite plans of destruction were exposed and Haman was hung at the gallows he had previously prepared for Mordecai!

How awesome it is when God turns the tables back upon our enemy. The Lord will use the weapons the enemy uses against God's chosen back upon the Amalekite. God's Word states that ALL things will work together for our good as we are called according to His purpose.

> *And we know that all things work together for good to them that love God, to them who are the called according to his purpose.*

Romans 8:28

The Esthers and Hamans Today

Esther was determined for destiny. She was a lady who knew God, knew the destiny of God's people and was willing to sacrifice her life for it. There are many Esthers in today's churches and ministries. However, they are also being greatly hindered by the Amalekite strongholds.

There are demonically inspired Hamans operating through manifestations of pride and arrogance. These spirits are reinforcing and protecting old **structures of religion**. Destiny cannot be accomplished without change for we are forever being "changed" (transformed) into God's image. The present day church is being challenged to move past religious mindsets and pursue God's Spirit. Religion is not relationship and never will be. Religion is a form and structure of beliefs and practices. However, simply having a form of beliefs will not replace a true relationship.

Many modern day Esthers are willing to sacrifice reputation, position and acceptance to approach the King and ask for His perfect will to be done. They will lay down their lives if necessary to pioneer a new truth. They are the ones who see into the future and destiny of the Church, they toss fear to the side, and who will die for the cause of Christ.

The Hamans of today will attempt to deceive many. They will proclaim that they are called by God to be the Aarons and Hurs, but all along they are jealous of authority and plot to destroy godly leaders. They work behind the scenes, secretly but steadily building gallows to hang and spiritually murder authority. They whisper false accusations to others in leadership and deceitfully approach the congregations in attempts to cause disunity. The Amalekites cohabitate with the accuser of the brethren. Together they plot coups and demonic "take-overs" for positions of authority. Many Hamans have wealth and use their financial status to control and manipulate; all to gain personal power in the decision processes.

The Amalekite spirit is in direct opposition to the plans and purposes of God. As Esther moved forward with godly focus, so must we. We must become even more determined for destiny so that we are empowered to thwart the plans of our enemies.

We must press into a greater level of intimacy with the Lord. Through our intimate times of fellowship and prayer, the Lord will speak strategies that will defeat the Amalekite spirit. God was faithful to Esther and He will also be faithful to us. He is a God of His Word and His promises to each of us are yes and amen. What the Lord promises, He will be faithful to fulfill.

Though the destiny thief seeks to destroy your promises, He will not steal the birthings of the Holy Spirit if you remain in intimacy. The seeds of your destiny will be fulfilled and He will rebuke the devourer for your sake! Though we may be weary in well doing, and there seems to be little strength to continue toward vision, He promises to bring the vision into reality.

God's Word states that He will not bring the seed (promise) to the time of birthing and not bring it fully forth.

And they said unto him, Thus saith Hezekiah, This day is a day of trouble, and of rebuke, and of blasphemy: for the children are come to the birth, and there is not strength to bring forth.

Is. 37:3

Shall I bring to the birth, and not cause to bring forth? saith the LORD: shall I cause to bring forth, and shut the womb? saith thy God.   Rejoice ye with Jerusalem, and be glad with her, all ye that love her: rejoice for joy with her, all ye that mourn for her: That ye may suck, and be satisfied with the breasts of her consolations; that ye may milk out, and be delighted with the abundance of her glory.

Is, 66:9-11

Chapter Ten

THE SEDUCTION OF THE RELIGIOUS SPIRIT

The sound of the phone ringing at two o'clock in the morning startled me from a deep sleep. My husband threw his arm toward the nightstand attempting to locate the light switch. He knocked the receiver onto the floor in his hasty attempt to answer the phone.

My heart began to pound. I realized it was the middle of the night, and mentally noted that phone calls at this hour are usually for emergencies.

"He-l-l-l-l-o." Barely awake Mickey answered the call. He went silent as he listened. It was my father. Mother was vomiting blood and they were rushing her to the emergency room.

My heart sank. *What? Why is she vomiting blood?* My husband assured me he did not understand either. We threw on clothing and met my parents at the hospital.

A series of tests proved that mother had lung cancer. The doctors scheduled surgery and removal of a third of both lungs. Though there was a malignant tumor in only one of the lungs, preventative measures were recommended for both; therefore both lungs would be surgically secured against future malignancy. Naturally, the entire family was devastated by the physician's report.

It was my sister, Pam who was the first to rise up in great faith. Her first words were in confidence that God would perform a miracle. The rest of the family, including my mother concurred. Though all of us were shaken in our faith, there was no way to look but UP at this point. We began to pray.

Another biopsy was scheduled in two days. The doctor released my mother to go home for two days for some down time. She would return to the hospital for the biopsy and then remain there for the surgery. It was during those two days that God began to speak to both of my parents and our entire family.

I remember being in mother's den, sitting on her sofa. My sister, Pam, began to share the healing power of the Lord and that it was God's will to heal her from cancer. I listened intently, watching Mother's face as she contemplated Pam's words. She and my father both began to nod their heads in agreement. Mother needed a miracle and we all knew it.

Pam laid hands upon Mother and prayed the prayer of faith. She had a measure of faith that even I needed. As she finished praying, I also began to pray. Together we bound the plans of the enemy and loosed God's healing touch upon her lungs. We cursed the cancerous tumor to the ROOT and commanded that root to dislodge from her lungs. We proclaimed her healing and reminded my mother of God's promises of healing.

I later drove home praying in tongues. I was worried, shaken and still trying to stand on God's promises. Her biopsy would be the next day. God will have to move, I reassured myself.

On the way to the hospital the next morning I was hindered by traffic jams. At every turn, I was delayed. I became more and more frustrated as I attempted to get to the hospital and be with my mother. Unfortunately, I arrived fifteen minutes late. I wanted to be with her during this crisis only to find myself getting further and further behind in arriving.

I finally reached the destination, hurried into the out-patient section and rushed to the second floor. Attempting to find the proper room, I noticed her doctor standing in the hallway. I stopped to ask if he was about to perform the procedure, thinking HE was running behind. Instead, I noticed him staring intently into a glass jar.

"Doctor," I inquired, "Have you already done the biopsy?"

No answer. Instead, he continued to stare into the jar of some type of clear solution. I moved in closer to see WHAT was in this jar. I noticed it looked strange and black. It had long tentacles or feelers of some type.

"I can't believe it." He said puzzlingly. "I simply can't believe it!"

"What?" I pushed for a clear answer.

The doctor was obviously stunned. He began to shake his head in total unbelief as to what had happened. "We just performed a biopsy of your mother's left lung. The tumor was even larger than I anticipated. It was "angry," which means it was definitely growing and malignant. When I began to scrape with the instrument used for a biopsy, your mother coughed abruptly. As she coughing, the tumor completely dislodged from her lung and ended up in this jar. I went in for a small biopsy and now the entire tumor is here in this jar!"

Still in total amazement, he continued. "Not only that, but where the tentacles of the tumor were, the lung immediately healed over with fresh pink skin. I looked again, and only fresh, pink, new tissue is there where the tumor was!"

Tears immediately filled my eyes and found their way down my face. God had done it, I thought to myself. God did it!

I glanced into the room and there was my mother still on the surgery table. Her hands were lifted into the air; she was praising God. She knew she had experienced a miracle. Over and over the words "thank you Jesus" found their way into the airways.

Suddenly, she jumped from off the table and began to run up and down the hallway of the second floor. My once reserved, Baptist little mother, who always hesitated to share her faith, was approaching EVERYONE on the floor with her testimony. "Jesus healed me! Jesus healed me!" she testified to everyone in her path!

The doctor smiled at her excitement. He didn't attempt to hinder her excitement. There was no attempt from the staff to point her toward the exit doors during her excitement....clearly all had witnessed a miracle.

"Here, you might want to keep this." The doctor said as he handed me a picture of the tumor confined in the jar. I looked for several minutes at the picture. Clearly, it was a demonic-looking "something!" It was a black tumor with very long feelers (tentacles) and roots. Obviously this tumor had attempted to permanently lodge itself and spread its deadly infection. As I focused on this miracle, the memory of Pam and cursing the tumor to the "root" ran through my mind. God had most definitely answered our request. He had removed that angry demonic tumor from the root....and now the enemy's plan was fully contained in a jar that had a closed lid on it! I still have the picture of that tumor. Periodically I retrieve it from the bureau, gaze upon it and am reminded of God's miracle working power!

Miracles Are for Today!

Miracles did not cease when the apostles died. A religious spirit will try to convince believers that it did. I had been taught that error for years when I attended a certain denominational church. When I began to understand the FULL gospel, I realized that God is the same, yesterday, today and forever! If He healed yesterday, He will heal today. My mother was proof of that. I also have proof of that. My sister has been healed of ovarian tumors several times. My mother died once of a heart attack while in an ambulance and God brought her back to life. He has miraculously resurrected my mother from the jaws of death at least five times. We have witnessed His faithfulness over and over.

God wants to do even more miracles through each of us. Just as He flowed through the apostles in instances documented throughout the scriptures, He desires to flow through today's believers. However, there is a stronghold of doubt and unbelief that hinders the greater levels of faith that are needed to flow in the miraculous.

Religious spirits were active during Jesus' ministry and continue to affect us today. Religious spirits are secure in "old order" and protest any new revelation from God. Religious spirits promote pride, arrogance and religious mindsets and these strongholds will work through people in local churches. This is the voice of a religious spirit speaking through people:

"I don't believe healing is for today."
"God doesn't perform miracles."
"We must pray for God's will, not a miracle."
"Speaking in tongues is of the devil."
"I don't believe in that holy-roller stuff."
"What do you mean you lay hands on the sick?"
"You mean your church services are over forty-five minutes long?"

OR IN A SPIRIT FILLED CONGREGATION THE RELIGIOUS SPIRIT
MAY SOUND LIKE THIS....

"I can hear from God better than the senior leader."

" I am a prophet of God, listen to ME"

"I alone hear God better than all. Hear ME only!"

"Women should be silent in the church!"

"There are no prophets or apostles today."

"We should not sing in the Spirit."

"I don't believe in spiritual warfare."

"I don't believe in deliverance. Jesus died on the cross to deliver me...even
    though I feel crazy at times!"

"The only anointed and true Word is the King James translation."

"Surely you don't DANCE in church, do you?"

"You actually CLAP in church?"

Those who operate in a religious spirit will contest and hinder major breakthroughs in the Spirit. There are many who are teaching cutting-edge, breakthrough revelations concerning the power of deliverance. However, there are
multitudes who totally disagree with the need for deliverance. This group be-
lieves that the blood of Jesus healed everything when they became born again.
They will profess that their attitudes and behavior do not necessitate deliverance,
yet they are bound up in shame, guilt, mental torment, addictions and various
forms of sickness.

The truth is that Jesus did die for our sins; however that is only one phase
of our blessing. There is more for us to walk into and experience - such as complete deliverance and complete salvation, which involves healing and whole-
ness. There are measures of physical breakthroughs and layers of deliverance
that can occur at different levels of spiritual maturity.

It is always amazing that those who protest deliverance need it the most.
Actually, a demon has convinced them that they don't need deliverance.

A religious spirit will always attempt to convince us to compromise. It
travels closely with seducing spirits and unclean spirits. The seducing spirit
seeks to seduce us into areas of sin and uncleanness together with doubt and

unbelief. These spirits bring defilement and apostasy. They work against our minds and feed thoughts such as:

"Go ahead and sin, no one will ever know."
"It was easier BEFORE you were a Christian."
"Go back into the world!"
"Go ahead, take a drink. God won't care!"
"Cheating on your wife is NOT the unpardonable sin!"

Just at the time of a major breakthrough the familiar voice of this seducing unclean spirit sounds like this:

"God doesn't really care about you. Give up."
"You're unworthy to receive any breakthrough. Throw in the towel now."
"You'll never receive a promise from God. Just look at you. You're unworthy and worthless."
"Why don't you just speak it out loud....God is a liar and you have been deceived with all this 'FAITH' stuff!"
"This mountain is TOO BIG for your God."

The New Wine

When God is bringing forth a new truth or a new move, the religious spirit will always rise up and manifest. Religious tradition will begin to dictate how God moves. If we allow God's Spirit to minister as He desires, it seems that we immediately are challenged to go back to what is comfortable and we "box-in" God. This is because He is moving differently than before, challenging our mindsets and comfort zones. Many pastors are so afraid of losing control they do not allow any tongues, prophecy or laying on of hands for healing and miracles. This is very sad because the Holy Spirit desires to speak and move freely, ministering life to us.

Religious Tradition Brings Death

Religious tradition is legalism and the Word says that the law brings death. Only the Spirit of God will release LIFE in a service.

Religious tradition and mindsets will dictate loss of faith and spiritual revelation.

There is a NEW WINE of the Spirit that God is releasing. When Jesus spoke on the new wine, He was attempting to break the disciples free of tradition and mindsets. In fact, He came to challenge them concerning their belief system and religious structures. Jesus was determined to provoke spirits of religion and tradition by working miracles and speaking truth! He knew that His present truth messages would cause a ripping and a tearing of their religious systems.

There must be new wineskins to hold this new wine. And there will be a ripping and a tearing until we choose to change. I have observed many areas of ripping and tearing within God's Church. New truths are being taught and it is causing people to be uncomfortable. Many are not allowing God to challenge them to change. Instead, they are bailing out and going back to "old things."

His Fire Burns Out Tradition

The fire is hot, the heat is hotter and God is purifying His church. A majority of His children only "think" they want the new wine - until they are challenged to change their "thinking!" God desires to move differently than before and this "new move" will challenge every mindset. IF WE EMBRACE THE FULL KINGDOM MESSAGE THERE WILL BE A FIRE! The fire is designed to burn away tradition, mindsets and old religious structure that does not present life.

One thing I have realized is that when His Spirit moves in the "New Thing" it WILL rip up and tear down the old religious order. As a pastor, when I observed this, I began to pray for new wineskins to receive fresh revelation. I fasted and prayed to AVOID the ripping and tearing. The Lord later spoke to me and said that in order for me to see that our church was not ready for the new move of the Spirit, He ALLOWED and actually CAUSED areas to rip and tear!

OH NO! I don't want ripping and tearing. Do YOU? No pastor in their right mind desires for the congregation to be ripped and torn apart. But let me confess to you...it did get my full attention. When I experienced this, I had to press into God and find out what truth we were not embracing. If God was pouring out new wine and there was a tearing....something needed fixing!!

Let Him Move!

This is probably happening to many other churches. Don't blame the devil! Press into God and ask Him how you can ACCOMMODATE the Holy Spirit more! When we ask the Holy Spirit to come into our meetings, let Him MOVE. If you're asking Him to come, and you're not ready for His fullness....it might rip and tear some things.

If you are NOT experiencing this in your life, your churches, or your ministry, don't despair! The enemy loves to place shame on God's chosen. Simply back off, seek God and ask Him to begin to speak clearly into areas He desires to change. All of us have control issues, but the Holy Spirit wants full control.

In every new area of Holy Spirit directed change you will be challenged with mindsets and religious tradition. Religious spirits will rise up against you. Jezebel spirits of control will attempt to control and manipulate your decisions. The accuser of the brethren will falsely testify against you. If these spirits begin to operate...you're probably on the right track! Don't quit now! Become determined for destiny! You're moving in the right direction and embracing new wine!

Jesus said that once someone has drunk the old wine, they do not want new wine. This is very true. Old habits die hard. Old belief systems die hard. We continually box God into a formula and yet we don't fully understand that though He does not change....He LOVES change! He is continually changing us into His image. To change us, He will change the order of our church services so that He can move in a greater dimension of His power!

Remember how the religious spirit operated against Jesus? The spirit instructed Jesus that He could not heal on the Sabbath, and that he could not eat with the sinners. The Pharisees were pious and prideful in their traditions but did not know God. The same spirit operates today in our modern churches. To find God we have to get past all the paraphernalia of idols, rituals, certain hymns and long lifeless prayers. All the while God is saying...."Wait a minute. I'd like to say something!"

Religion says that we have to speak a certain way, pray a certain way, believe a certain way, confess a certain way, proclaim a certain way....even prophesy a certain way! One can be CERTAIN of only one thing....God wants control and He is causing a ripping and tearing in the church wineskins. This is all due to a needed wake up call; God wants to bring change. I pray for the grace of God for each of us as He leads us into all truth.

Several years ago a gentleman approached me because I used a different translation of the Bible other than the King James. Most of the time, I teach from the King James, but for the congregation I used another translation for greater clarity. Immediately after the service he told me that God only approved the King James and that I was teaching deception. This is the voice of a religious stronghold at work attempting to bind up the Body of Christ with legalism. As I stated before, the law brings death and the Spirit of God releases life and empowerment.

Witchcraft and the Religious Spirit

Religious spirits often manifest through witchcraft. (By now you are realizing that witchcraft is a manifestation of ALL seducing spirits.) Witchcraft is a work of the flesh and is forbidden in the scriptures. We are instructed to never partake of any form of witchcraft; however many of us do not realize that rebellion is also witchcraft.

An intercessor with a religious spirit will often pray soulish prayers targeted against a leader. Often, deceived intercessors feel that they get the proper direction for the Church. They attempt to force their "direction received through prayer" upon the leadership. If the leadership is not ready to move out on the unction of the intercessor, he/she will at times feel rejected and angry. Rather than submit, the intercessor will pray their own will out of rebellion and lack of submission to delegated authority.

Though motives, in the beginning, may have been innocent, the prayers have taken on a form of charismatic witchcraft. Charismatic witchcraft is the term assigned to soulish "wishions" which are prayed. It is prayer based upon an individual's isolated and personal insight, desire and will. This form of witchcraft will hinder godly authority and a move of the Holy Spirit. If you are an intercessor please remember to remain accountable and teachable. Do not allow a religious, judgmental stronghold to overtake you whenever God is releasing change and transformation. (For more information on charismatic witchcraft, I recommend Gary Greenwald's book, *Seductions Exposed*.)

For rebellion is as the sin of witchcraft, and stubbornness is as in-
iquity and idolatry. Because thou hast rejected the word of the
LORD, he hath also rejected thee from being king.

1 Samuel 15:23

How often have we been as the Apostle Paul and have kicked against God's plans? When we resist His directions and instructions we are in rebellion....witchcraft! However, there are genuine witches and sorcerers that pray against churches and ministers. Forms of incantations and satanic rituals are practiced that attempt to hinder the plans and purposes of God. Satan has principalities and powers at work against God's Church. Many different spiritual assignments are released through demons attempting to abort the plans and purposes of God's chosen. We must all guard ourselves against rebelling against God's leaders and those He has assigned over us. To rebel against those God has placed in authority opens the doors to many demonic assignments.

Evil Reports Against Others

Religious spirits will team up with the accuser of the brethren to speak evil reports concerning others, especially against leadership. As God is pouring out His new wine, if there is negativity in the midst, your wineskin will begin to rip and tear. His truth will not compete with old mindsets and tradition. Negativity will stop a fresh move of the Spirit because negativity gives place to doubt and unbelief. God will always honor faith. Doubt and unbelief aborts breakthroughs planned by the Spirit.

Once evil reports are released, defilement follows. Remember, we are to not touch the unclean thing? If we open the door to defilement, we open doors to unclean spirits (discussed later).

An evil report involves false accusation, a distortion of facts and bogus information. Most of the time these falsehoods are communicated with wrong motives intended to cause harm to someone or their reputations. At first it may be received in total innocence but if repeated, it later brings contamination. An evil report is similar to an evil germ that becomes active upon infection. If not treated, the infection moves into a disease and possible death. The same happens to us when we partake of evil reports. Whether we "receive" the report or "give" the report, the defilement is the same.

Evil reports take the form of gossip, whispering, slander, backbiting, tale bearing and being a busybody. Reports often develop from deep wounds, jealousy, bitterness, rebellion, envy and pride. Those who have been wounded by authority are often bitter and begin to speak negatively about leaders with hurtful intent. Often, there is jealousy in the Body of Christ and some become faultfinders.

Once defilement occurs, symptoms of disease begin to develop. Symptoms of the infection are:

1. believing the evil reports to be true without going to the correct sources for truth.
2. forming negative opinions and spreading rumors
3. judging others based on a negative report
4. focusing on the negative in other areas

The above symptoms left untreated may result in disease. Did you realize that bitterness causes physical illness? I knew a man who was extremely full of bitterness. He refused to move forward beyond a victimization mentality. He was struck with severe arthritis. The Lord gave me a word of knowledge concerning his bitterness and unforgiveness. After he received truth, the Lord delivered him from the demonic oppression caused by the bitterness and unforgiveness and he was healed!

The Bible warns us to be consistent to forgive those who have hurt us. Forgiveness releases the love of God and the fruits of healing to our hearts and bodies.

If in your heart you feel the urge to spread negative reports and you find yourself bitter, it is then time to begin to repent. Ask for forgiveness for listening to lies and negativity. Ask the Lord to forgive you for allowing that evil spirit to work through you. You will know that your heart is cleansed whenever you begin to grieve over negative reports. You will become saddened to hear negative words spoken about leaders or those you respect and admire. By quickly examining our own lives for failures, we will most often derail any of satan's plans to use us in this fashion again.

Destiny vs. Negative Reports

We will never reach destiny if we choose to believe negative reports. The only way to move forth into our destiny is to believe God and His Word. This involves believing what He says about <u>others and us</u>! Rather than remaining critical of others, begin confessing what God has declared over their lives. Believe me; it will make a difference in your heart! Soon you will notice your attitude (and motive) toward them changing!

Life penetrates our bodies and minds when we choose to believe the Words of God. Defilement and death are the results of negative reports. Be on guard, dear one. The enemy goes forth as a roaring lion to devour you! Choose to believe the Lord and experience your victory!

Have the spirit of Joshua and Caleb. You have a higher calling, a destiny to fulfill in God. Do not allow any area of defilement or uncleanness to dictate your life. Begin NOW to believe God's Word and utterly destroy all. You CAN go in and possess your promise!

Has the religious spirit had a stronghold over your life? If so, then how?

Below, write a strategy of how you plan to overcome and fulfill your destiny.

Repent from having mindsets concerning the move of the Holy Spirit. Receive empowerment from the Holy Spirit to claim and possess your mountain of promise.

Are you struggling with loving others? If so, write below what God has said concerning them. After writing down the positive reports from the Lord, pray over each scripture asking God to heal your heart toward them.

Chapter Eleven

THE SEDUCTION OF THE UNCLEAN SPIRIT

*And there was in their synagogue a man with an unclean spirit; and he cried out, Saying, **Let us alone**; what have we to do with thee, thou Jesus of Nazareth? At thou come to destroy us? I know thee who thou art, the Holy One of God.*

Mark 1:23-24

nclean spirits want us to leave them alone. These demonic spirits desire to continue defiling God's people, influencing them to continue their present sin, especially spiritual adultery.

When we think of someone being *unclean* we often describe them as being "dirty, nasty," and even at times "untouchable" due to the filth they may have been exposed to. The Webster's Dictionary defines *unclean* as "being morally or spiritually impure." It goes further to say that it also means being "infected with a harmful supernatural contagion." [27] This is very interesting, because the instructions from God have always been to ***touch not the unclean thing*** (2 Corinthians 6:17). We are instructed to remove ourselves from every *unclean* influence and become holy and blameless before the Lord.

The unclean spirit is a tremendous stronghold in the Body of Christ. Sin causes defilement and defilement closes the doors to spiritual breakthroughs. This is the very reason that the unclean spirits continue to cry out "*Leave us alone!*" The spirits will persuade us into believing that there is no power in the name of Jesus, and especially that there is no need for <u>deliverance</u>. Unclean spirits know the name of Jesus and that's why their goal is to deceive many into believing that they don't need deliverance. The devil is a liar and a deceiver, we must begin to compare our thought patterns and beliefs to the Word of God.

Many people have asked me how I know when an unclean spirit is in operation. The main way I have determined the spirit at work is by the gift of spiritual discernment. With proper discernment any spirit is recognized. However, there are certain characteristics that are common when an unclean spirit is manifesting within a church congregation or individuals.

Characteristics of the Unclean Spirit

1.   <u>Unkept appearance and defiled speech</u>

The most obvious to the natural eye is also a representation of the actual unclean spirit at work; this is when there is a lack of personal hygiene. Individuals will appear "unkept" in their appearance and appear dirty or filthy. Often, cursing or telling dirty jokes defiles their speech.

2.   <u>Lust, sexual perversion and pornography</u>

One can recognize an unclean spirit where there is lust and perversion. Many times pornography is a stronghold as well as sexual deviation. Incest, adultery, masturbation and twisted perverted imaginations are included when an unclean spirit is working within someone's life.

I have visited homes that were so unkept that I wanted to quickly leave the premises. Obviously, to the natural eye it was uclean, but most of the time an unclean spirit has become a <u>stronghold in the home</u>. When there is a continual pattern of natural uncleanness, it is a spiritual root.

3. Rigid belief systems

Within a congregation an unclean spirit manifests somewhat differently. Jesus addressed the Pharisees as being unclean due to their **belief system**. He said that one is defiled not by what is eaten, but because of what is on the inside. The Pharisees believed and trusted in their religious order. They trusted in their fasting, long senseless prayers and religious structure.

4. Doubt and unbelief

The Jewish believers were saturated with doubt and unbelief and Jesus continually rebuked them for their lack of faith. Jesus addressed these "religious" men as a den of vipers and unclean. In Matthew 12:33-34 Jesus told the religious leaders that they were evil and had been **corrupted**. He specifically addressed them as having corrupt and rotten (defiled) fruit. We know that if the fruit is corrupt and defiled then the entire tree is corrupt. In other words there was an evil spirit, a strong territorial spirit over the religious system at that time.

5. It is a regional (territorial) stronghold

An unclean spirit is a "regional stronghold" and most often involves a large region or territory with its demonic influence. Jesus dealt with the unclean spirit in the region of the Decapolis, which was composed of several cities. While in that one region he cast out the unclean devils. It is very important that we recognize its influence as it gains demonic governmental control over large areas at a time.

When this spirit moves into its assigned district, it takes over entire families, neighborhoods, cities and even states and countries. When it targets a local church there could be many in the congregation who might manifest unclean thoughts, areas of sexual defilement, perversion and sexual addictions, even sickness and disease. It will also manifest in congregational doubt and unbelief that hinder church breakthrough.

6. Old behavior patterns, dead places, bondage and mental torment

The unclean spirit desires to contain believers in old patterns and dead places or areas that are defiled. Stagnant waters breed mosquitoes and these insects suck the life giving-blood from its victims. When the Body of Christ chooses to remain stagnant, they are open prey to the enemy. These gruesome insects will begin to steal the life from them. In order to avoid these bloodsuckers we must keep moving! MOVE and ADVANCE FORWARD! When we stop moving as God directs, we are in danger of defilement. In fact, we easily move into rebellion and rebellion opens doors to witchcraft and many other demonic spirits.

Observe the documentation of the unclean spirit that lived in the tombs:

> *And when he was come out of the ship, immediately there met him out of the tombs a man with an **unclean spirit**, Who had his dwelling among the tombs; and no man could bind him, no, not with chains: Because that he had been often **bound** with fetters and chains, and the chains had been plucked asunder by him, and the fetters broken in pieces: neither could any man tame him.*

Mark 5:2-4 (emphasis mine)

Notice that this man with the unclean spirit lived in the tombs, a place of death and decay. Unclean spirits desire to keep us bound spiritually. The demoniac was mentally tormented and no man could speak reasoning to him. He was completely controlled by an unclean spirit. The Scripture goes on to say that he would cry night and day and literally cut himself with stones. I have pastored women who have been so tormented by the unclean spirit that they have cut themselves with knives and other sharp instruments just as the man with the unclean spirit. When this spirit invades a congregation, the cutting can be different. **The Christians actually go after each other!** They will use cutting words against the leadership. They will falsely accuse each other and say words that "cut deep" into the hearts of others.

7. Words of death and evil reports

Life and death are in the power of the tongue; therefore many words of death are released when an unclean spirit is active. Words easily become curses and death assignments when fueled with jealousy, hatred and rage; all manifestations of an unclean spirit. Life and death are in the power of the tongue; be cautious what you speak and release to others.

*Death and life are in the power of the tongue: and they that love it
shall eat the fruit thereof.*

Proverbs 18:21

Unclean spirits cause us to focus on the faults of others rather than
searching for areas of our own personal defilement. When we begin to become
negative, lash out verbally, and disconnect, there is most likely an unclean spirit
in the midst. Believers need to continually search their hearts for areas of defilement. Remember, Jesus stated that it was not so much the uncleanliness on
the outside, but the inside that defiled the man.

8.   Aborts and separates destiny

Unclean spirits **separate** us from our destiny. The unclean spirit separated the
man and placed him in a graveyard, where no one wanted to live. The man lived
alone and became crazy and lonely. The unclean spirit will convince Christians
that they do not fit, do not belong. The spirit devises plans to cause offenses
attempting to separate us from spiritual authority and like believers. The scripture says that where there is unity there is life. Therefore dead places promote
disunity and separation. Whenever an unclean spirit attacks a church congregation the first area I notice is the disunity among the people. Then the next area is
the dismantling of authority within the congregation. Slanderous words are
hurled against the leaders and then there is a breakdown in the spiritual covering
and people begin to disconnect. Suddenly, there is a breech among the brethren
and the lack of trust in leadership causes an exodus or possible church split. If
believers do not lock back into God's plan, their destiny is aborted.

9.   Unclean spirits travel with their companions

Unclean spirits often travel with a multitude of other spirits. The demon-
possessed man in the tombs was controlled by a demon that identified himself as
Legion indicating there were many demons at work. I have discerned that unclean spirits often travel with the Jezebel and Absalom spirits and religious spirits. Absalom spirits promote disunity and slander against true godly authority.
Jezebel promotes idolatry, false belief systems, fornication and sexual perversion. All of these sins will stain the Body of Christ with sin and defilement.

10. Spirit of death, sickness and disease and generational patterns

Death, sickness and disease will often become continual problems when an unclean spirit attacks a church or family. Where there is a generational stronghold of an unclean spirit, you most often find long-standing disease and repeated acts of sexual perversion. Children are influenced with a generational pattern of the unclean spirit manifesting as masturbation, pornography and foul language. When it attacks a generation the stronghold remains intact until it is bound up and then broken off through prayer and deliverance.

Several years ago I had a dream concerning an unclean spirit. At the time of the dream, our church congregation was experiencing much turmoil. I discerned that an unclean spirit was attacking the young adults. I quickly went to prayer to discern how to dismantle the false authority of the defiling spirit. The Lord answered me with a dream. The dream was about a strongman who had a spirit similar to Saul in the Old Testament. The strongman lived in a very dark castle and he rode a black horse. The strongman was fully dressed in armor. In the dream the "Saul" spirit spoke to me and said that he had a plan to destroy ALL of Israel. Then I awoke.

Since I travel and teach on dreams and visions and their interpretations, this particular dream was very easy for me to interpret. The dark castle represented a stronghold of darkness. The spirit of Saul represented the old religious order, the old way. Horses most often represent strength. In this case, it was a dark horse, which represented the strength of darkness. Since Saul had on full armor, I knew it represented warfare. He proclaimed that this attack was not simply against our small congregation but rather it was an attack against ALL Israel. In other words, it was a regional attack!

My husband and I are an apostolic-prophetic team who apostolically oversee several churches and regions for Christian International Ministries. At the time of the dream we were one week away from hosting a large prophetic conference in Dallas, Texas. We began to alert the entire region concerning the dream; we warned them against any possible manifestations concerning the unclean spirit. The entire network in Texas began to fast and pray. At the time of the conference we experienced a powerful manifestation of God's presence. We corporately bound the unclean spirit over our state and loosed God's prophetic-

apostolic mantle. It was one of the most powerful conferences we ever hosted!
The plans against our congregation ceased quickly after the conference was over
and we proceeded toward destiny in His purposes. Hallelujah!

11. Robs faith and determination

An unclean spirit will rob your determination for destiny! It will separate and
isolate you and then begin to wear you out! In the past, when I had been under
an evil assignment from an unclean spirit, I would be absolutely exhausted. As
a result of being physically drained I would become ill. This is the enemy's plan
to cause burnout, fatigue and illness.

Again, remember, the enemy's job is to wear out the saints. He will target
with whatever stronghold will gain victory, will isolate you from the Body, and
then will move in for the kill. This is why it is very important to remain connected to the Body when under attack. If we become separated we are then an
easy prey for the enemy.

12. Separates from destiny links and causes loss of vision

If the unclean stronghold succeeds at separating you from the rest of the Body,
or separating you from your destiny links it will then cause you to lose vision.
Vision only comes when we are connected. When we become disconnected, it
is too easy to lose focus and lose vision and then we will perish. Life and vital-
ity are the fruits of pursuing vision. When there is no vision there is no energy to
go forth and accomplish destiny.

> *And the LORD answered me, and said, Write the vision, and make
> it plain upon tables, that **he may run** that readeth it. For the vision
> is yet for an appointed time, but at the end it shall speak, and not
> lie: though it tarry, wait for it; because it will surely come, it will
> not tarry.*
>
> Habakkuk 2:2-3 (my emphasis)

Driving Out the Unclean Spirit

Since doubt and unbelief will always manifest when an unclean spirit is in
the midst, the way to uproot its power and entanglement is to begin to speak

God's Word in FAITH. Fear will attempt to enter into the hearts of man when this spirit is at work, however take a firm stand and remain in faith.

In Luke 9:37-42 the Scripture documents the disciples attempting to drive an unclean spirit out from a child. As they tried to cast it out, they could not. Instead the spirit tore at the child and caused foaming at the mouth. Jesus boldly addressed their **lack of faith** and called the disciples **perverse**.

> *And Jesus answering said, O __faithless__ and __perverse__ generation, how long shall I be with you, and suffer you? Bring thy son hither. (Verse 41)*

One of the first areas I noticed concerning this passage was that the disciples dealt with doubt and unbelief when they attempted to cast out the unclean spirit. This confirms my hypothesis that doubt and unbelief will manifest when this stronghold attacks.

Jesus addressed them as not only faithless but *perverse* as well. How interesting, I thought, as I studied the effects of the unclean spirit. The word *perverse* in this passage translates as being distorted and to turn aside (from the right path through corruption) and oppose or plot against the saving purposes and plans of God![28] One can easily see by this translation how the unclean spirit causes its victim to turn away from destiny and oppose the purposes and plans that God has for us!

It will take clean hands and pure hearts to totally destroy the unclean spirit. At times, as pastors, we have called our entire congregation to fasting and prayer. We have cleansed our land by praying over the church property. We have continuously repented from generational curses or any areas of defilement the Lord reveals. One season we fasted and prayed and then called the intercessors together as we poured oil upon our property. We sprinkled salt upon the earth symbolizing purity and cleansing of our land.

Clean hands represent freedom from guilt, innocence, blameless and cut-off from sin. As we repented, we were cleansing ourselves from iniquities and curses from past generations. We prayed that the Lord would cleanse and purify our hearts so that we could experience a higher level of His glory. The only way for us to ascend to a higher level and experience His greater presence was through the cleansing of our hearts and hands.

Who shall ascend into the hill of the LORD? Or who shall stand in his holy place? He that hath clean hands, and a pure heart; who hath not lifted up his soul unto vanity, nor sworn deceitfully. He shall receive the blessing from the LORD, and righteousness from the God of his salvation.   This is the generation of them that seek him, that seek thy face, O Jacob. Selah.

Ps 24:3-6

Freedom From An Unclean Spirit Depends Upon These Actions:

R ecognize it for what it is: Defilement!

R epent for all areas of the defilement.

R emember His Word and ways to insure proper cleansing and healing.

R ightousness is the right choice.

R eel in your thoughts.

R enew your mind.

R egard righteous living as a necessity.

AND UTTERLY DESTROY ALL

Don't Look Back!

It is very important to not look back. When God delivered Lot and his family from Sodom and Gomorrah they were not to look back. The result was the destructions of Lot's wife...she just couldn't let go of the old thing!

God is calling you out! When He calls you away from an old lifestyle, a city, or a relationship you cannot look back over your shoulder.   Let go and separate yourself unto Him and He will be faithful to save you.

Are there areas of defilement in your life? Take time right now to repent of your sin. Repentance will cleanse you from all unrighteousness. Sanctify yourself by the washing of His powerful Word.

Chapter Twelve

THE JEZEBEL SPIRIT

I felt a chill run down my spine as she approached the altar.

Oh no! I told the Lord; surely she doesn't have ANOTHER prophetic word!

She moved in for the kill, searching for a microphone. She stared straight at me, as if to intimidate me with her determination and imagined anointing. She bowed up her back, almost like an attacking cat and stretching out her hand to get the microphone. She said "I have a word from God!"

I held my position as senior leader and Pastor of our flock and began searching for an inner witness if I should allow her to prophesy. The intimidation from the Jezebel spirit arose to undermine my authority.

I knew the season had come when Mickey and I had to say *"No"* to her. Though we had tried on numerous occasions to speak into her life and bring loving correction, the counsel was never received. Each time we had attempted to bring needed adjustments there was heavy retaliation. Based on past history I knew that after I maintained my godly position and refused to allow her to prophesy "in the flesh" she would cause strife and division within minutes after her rejection.

I fought through my fears of long counseling sessions with her friends in the church, betrayal, lies and witchcraft words and said "No, not this time."

Her cold eyes stared through me. She was not smiling and was definitely unhappy. This was truly the straw that broke the camel's back. She did not receive the microphone, but that did not hinder her determination to speak her mind.......words that did not bear witness in the least began to flow out of her mouth. Then, she prayed aloud in the spirit.... it was not the Spirit of God speaking. The false tongue bore no witness and there was no godly interpretation.

Though she would have enjoyed more attention by giving false direction through illegitimate authority, Mickey grabbed the microphone and took godly authority. She removed herself, went to her seat and snatched her children and husband from their seats. They all exited out the front doors.

The atmosphere was disturbed...actually defiled. A false prophetess had been in the House of God attempting to usurp authority and gain illegal authority. It had been a seven-month battle with a strong Jezebel spirit. Hopefully, now it was over.

After the service, I was extremely grieved. I prayed, I repented, and I mourned over this relationship. *Why couldn't I help her? We tried every way possible to bring healing and restoration.* I cried out for answers.

A few days later we experienced another fall-out with several couples leaving with her. The Jezebel gathered her flock, which she had controlled and they left for their new church. It had been a pattern for this group moving from church to church; with Jezebel seeking a position of authority. The group entered into the next place wounded and unhealed and ultimately left the next church the same way they entered....wounded and unhealed. This is because Jezebel will not receive correction and discipline. If this spirit cannot control a pastor and congregation it will not remain. A Jezebel seeks only those who can be controlled and manipulated.

Though it was sad to lose families, there was nothing left for us to do except to release them. We had a clear word from the Lord that we were to no longer tolerate Jezebel's intimidation and control. In fact, God reminded us of His strict words to the Church in Thyatira, which he rebuked for tolerating Jezebel:

18) And unto the angel of the church in Thyatira write; These things saith the Son of God, who hath his eyes like unto a flame of fire, and his feet are like fine brass; 19) I know thy works, and charity, and service, and faith, and thy patience, and thy works; and the last to be more than the first. 20) **<u>Notwithstanding I have a few things against thee, because thou sufferest that woman Jezebel,</u>** *which calleth herself a prophetess, to teach and to* **<u>seduce</u>** *my servants to commit fornication, and to eat things sacrificed unto idols. 21) And I gave her space to repent of her fornication; and* **<u>she repented not</u>**. *22) Behold, I will cast her into a bed, and them that commit adultery with her into great tribulation, except they repent of their deeds. 23) And I will kill her children with death; and all the churches shall know that I am he which searcheth the reins and hearts: and I will give unto every one of you according to your works. 24) But unto you I say, and unto the rest in Thyatira, as many as have not this doctrine, and which have not known the depths of Satan, as they speak; I will put upon you none other burden.*

Revelation 2:18-24 (emphasis mine)

Jezebel and Her Seductions

We must search the scriptures to understand the characteristics of a Jezebel spirit. Jezebel is mentioned in both the Old and New Testaments. In the Old Testament she was known as Jezebel, the queen, who attacked and murdered the prophets of God (1 Kings 18:4). We see her name mentioned again in the New Testament (Rev 2:18). It is obvious that it is not the same woman from the Old Testament, but rather the scriptures are speaking of the "spirit" of Jezebel, which was operating within the church. This same spirit operates through others today; infecting churches with its manipulation and control.

In the Old Testament we read how Jezebel **murdered** the prophets and **intimidated** Elijah to the point that he wanted to die! When she threatened to kill him, he ran into the wilderness and hid in a cave. God had to call Elijah out from that dark place, speak life and direction to him, and empower him to move forward. Otherwise, the threat of Jezebel was so intimidating Elijah may have spent the rest of his days in hiding.

Believe me; I have had the same battle with Jezebel myself! The seducing spirit of Jezebel promotes what Bishop Hamon refers to as the "Persecution Complex." In his book, *Prophets, Pitfalls, and Principles,*[29] Bishop Bill Hamon exposes the intimidation and persecution that Elijah experienced. It was so strong that Elijah developed a persecution complex; which is the deception of being so overwhelmingly persecuted that one can run away from their destiny! Elijah had a destiny to hold steadfast and remain in his spiritual authority in the region. However, when Jezebel came after him, he left his post, took the risk of aborting his destiny and ran in the opposite direction!

Do you remember the story? In 1 Kings 18 it is documented that Elijah called down fire from heaven, slew the false prophets of Baal, prophesied and released rain after years of drought and then outran Ahab's chariot into the entrance of Jezreel. Then in the very next chapter Jezebel was wroth and threatened to murder Elijah for all he had done! Instead of destroying Jezebel, as he had the false prophets he took off running for his life! Talk about a spirit of intimidation in operation! You would think that after Elijah had just been empowered by God to destroy the altars of Baal and then chop off the heads of hundreds of false prophets that he would remain CONFIDENT in his abilities! However, just one woman's message, of threatening and intimidating words, sent him off to a twenty-four hour trip...non-stop...into the wilderness! (See 1 Kings 19:1-4)

Have you been like me; had an incredible meeting or breakthrough only to find Jezebel knocking at your door? You answer the door only to be greeted with intimidation, false accusations, fear, manipulation, control and might I add seduction? I am referring to the seducing spirit of Jezebel, which pulls us out of our divine destiny. Yes, the Jezebel spirit isolates us from our destiny links and our destiny.

A key to Jezebel's tactic is the ability to understand just HOW Elijah received her threatening words. By closely examining verse 3, we see that he actually **ENVISIONED** his death! I have documented this passage for further inspection:

2) Then Jezebel sent a messenger unto Elijah, saying, So let the gods do to me and more also, if I make not thy life of one of them

*by tomorrow about this time. 3) And when Elijah **saw that,** he*
arose and went for his life...

1 Kings 19:2-3 (emphasis mine)

Notice the emphasis here: Elijah *saw* his destruction! He placed a "picture" with her intimidating words and his "seeing the destruction" sent him running!

Jezebel's words are directed at a seduction that steals destiny. Her intimidating threats take a firm grip not only upon our emotions but also our **minds!** The mental torment is so strong that we envision defeat, hopelessness and despair ***BEFORE*** it even happens! The results of her threatening words could be the same for us:

1. experiencing an overwhelming fear of dread and despair

2. running from our destiny

3. finding ourselves in the wilderness wishing to die

4. being **exhausted** due to the mental torment and running the opposite direction of destiny

5. finding ourselves in another 40 day and 40 night experience where God is calling us out of the cave! (see v. 4-9)

In the Old Testament the Jezebel spirit is shown as:

A murderer
A thief
An intimidator
A manipulator
A seducer
A controller
A liar
An idol worshiper
A promoter of illegitimate authority
A very strong woman who married an AHAB

In the New Testament God refers to her as (Rev 2:18-20)

A false prophetess
A false teacher
A seducer
A fornicator
An adulteress

You might be wondering how Jezebel is tolerated in today's churches. Don't simply look for a strong, controlling seductive woman...the Jezebel spirit has NO GENDER. The spirit of Jezebel will operate through male or female...anyone who allows it to control and use him/her will be the puppet of Jezebel.

In his book, *The Prophetic Fall of the Islamic Regime,* Glenn Miller writes on the power of principalities. He goes into length exposing the structures of the demonic kingdom and the satanic hierarchies. He states that:

"Principalities work through personalities. Personalities influence people. And people destroy other people."[30]

This holds true for the characteristics of a Jezebel spirit. Every Jezebel has an Ahab who co-labors with her in manipulation and control. Whether the spirit is married to an Ahab or has a ministry relationship with one; Jezebel will find SOMEONE to work through. The Jezebel-Ahab team is at times an overpowering duo of such intimidation that many times senior leaders and entire congregations will bow their hearts to the threats and control. Saints, God has already stated that we are NOT to tolerate this type of seduction! (See once again Rev. 2:20)

Desiring Position

A Jezebel spirit will desire to teach, especially before a proven time of trustworthiness. This spirit always pushes ahead and will intimidate leaders to gain her position. The spirit will also be very attracted to the prophetic ministry. Attempting also to control intercession, the spirit will falsely prophesy visions and words to control intercession and prayer…thus releasing witchcraft prayers upon others.

The spirit will always seduce others into her control by using false flattering words. The spirit will say things like:

> You can prophesy better than her…you should be the prophetess of the house.
>
> You are a more anointed intercessor than him…you should be the head intercessor.
>
> You're a much better teacher than her….you are so much more anointed and gifted than she is!

These flattering words appeal to PRIDE and are an attempt to gain a following. Their purpose is to draw and seduce others unto her in order to gain illegitimate power and authority. Jezebel desires total control; she will not remain in a place (or relationship) that she cannot control or manipulate.

Jezebel attracts people with "soulish" connections…what I refer to an ungodly "soul ties." These are relationships of extreme co-dependency…an unnatural "needing" of one another and an emotional dependence. The spirit "binds" you to itself, so tightly that you feel bound in loyalty…in fact you feel that you will never be free even if you try.

I noticed that when I would war against Jezebel, I would be exhausted most of the time. This is because of all the soulish prayers that were prayed, which were forms of charismatic witchcraft based on her selfish desires. Remember, witchcraft is a form of **control**, which is one of the main manifestations of Jezebel.

Control and Manipulation

Her name is translated as *without cohabitation* meaning that she will not submit or cohabitate with anyone. This further implies that she will not dwell (work along side) with anyone she cannot control or manipulate, and works against unity in any form. Jezebel is totally self centered and self-serving.

Once again, the Lord is quite clear that we are not to tolerate this spirit in our lives, our families, our churches nor our cities and nations.

I have had many dreams about a false prophet. In the dream the false voice was prophesying over my life. I would awaken, rebuke any curses from the enemy, and go back to sleep. One day I received the revelation of the dream. The Lord said that the false prophet in my dream was a stronghold of Jezebel. I argued with the Lord immediately, reminding him "I'm NOT a Jezebel!" (Well, wouldn't you argue with God about that?) Then, finally, I stopped defending myself and examined my heart. A soft voice spoke, "Sandie, what about idolatry? You have tried to maintain control all your life. You have desired your own will at times. This opened the door to idolatry and Jezebel was an idolater."

My mouth must have dropped to the floor! Talk about fast repentance.....I knew the areas He was correcting.... *"Father, forgive me. I repent of all control. Empower me to utterly destroy all...."*

Summarizing Jezebel:

1. Controls through flattery
2. Attempts to manipulate and control through false prophecy
3. Will always attract the weak and co-dependent
4. Operates in confusion
5. Manipulates to get her way
6. Seeks position and power
7. Dislikes repentance
8. Promotes idolatry
9. Always attracted to false government
10. Dislikes authority
11. Stirs up strife and division
12. Operates fully in an atmosphere of frustration, fear and intimidation

Dear ones, we are well able to slay the giant of Jezebel, which aborts our destiny! Below I have listed ways to defeat Jezebel. As I have stated before, repentance always brings breakthrough. So if you have opened any doors and allowed any entrance to Jezebel, then take this opportunity to repent.

Also, it is important to remember that it took a **Jehu** to destroy Jezebel. Therefore, I have concluded this chapter with the characteristics of Jehu to empower you to rise up and believe for a spiritual impartation to destroy your enemy!

How to Defeat Jezebel:

1. **Repent!** (Since the scripture says that Jezebel never repented…she doesn't want you to repent either.)
2. Immediately separate yourself from this spirit/person
3. Remain submitted to delegated godly authority
4. Remain teachable and accountable to authority
5. Replace all fear with great faith
6. Become a prayer warrior and spiritually alert
7. Develop and rely on your spiritual gift of discernment
8. Remove yourself from all idolatry
9. Seek servanthood over positions and titles
10. Do not seek out an Ahab!
11. Develop a spirit of Jehu
12. Continue to use your spiritual authority, using the keys of the kingdom to bind and loose the power of the enemy. Remember, YOU are seated in a place of authority with Christ Jesus. (See Eph 2:6)

Characteristics of Jehu (who defeated Jezebel)

1. He was a commander:
  (command the demonic stronghold to GO!

2. He was a conqueror.
  (conquer Jezebel with repentance and with the spirit of Jehu)

3. He was anointed
  (endure the processes of God to increase your anointing)

4. He was determined to achieve his destiny
  (be like Christ and set your face like flint toward your destiny)\

5. He had a calling to "smite" his enemy...he utterly destroyed all!

(Saul failed to smite the Amalekites, but Jehu fulfilled His commission. In 2 Kings 9:7 it says that God called him to *smite the house of Ahab.*)

6. He slew the false prophets, tore down the false idols and halted false prophecy.

(renew your mind and tear down all exalted imaginations)

7. He used "full strength" against his enemy.

(we notice in see 2 Kings 9:24 that ...*Jehu drew a bow with his full strength, and **smote** Jehoram...*)

8. He pursued his enemies.

(*Pursue* means that he followed in order to overtake and continued in order to accomplish (See 2 Kings 9:27). Just like King David, when he realized that his destiny was to *pursue* his enemy (the Amalekites) he was empowered to *overtake and recover all!* (See 1 Sa 13:8-9).

Chapter Thirteen

Destroying the Seeds of the Generations: The Spirit of Athaliah

We must not overlook the seed from Jezebel's generation!

he word "generation" means an offspring, a period of time, or a group of individuals belonging to a specific category at the same time. It is also referred to as a "life cycle."[31] A "cycle" relates to a recurring series of events or a repetition.

God has promised to each of us complete deliverance from the sins of our previous generations. He has also given us His Word that states that our generations will be protected. Prophetically, we are in a season when we are coming "full circle" facing old patterns of behavior. This is because it is time for a shift into the new place God has for us. It is our destiny to move forth and break free from tradition and mindsets. Much of what still hinders our spiritual growth has been mindsets passed from one generation to another. Since the same strongholds of Jezebel (control, manipulation, idolatry, etc.) have repeated themselves from one generation to another, the Lord is exhorting us to break agreements we have made with the spirit of Jezebel and any behaviors influenced by the Jezebel spirit.

Praying against the Jezebel spirit is most definitely needed to halt planned seductions from our enemy; however, we must not stop there. To insure total victory over spiritual seduction, we are required to consider her generational seed in order to utterly destroy all! This means that we will have to destroy the generations of Jezebel.

Athaliah: "Whom God Afflicts"

Jezebel had a daughter named Athaliah who was twice as vicious and determined to destroy the anointed of God. Being an offspring of both Ahab and Jezebel resulted in a double-demonic influence which operated in Judah. Some theologians believe that Athaliah was the actual daughter of Jezebel and Ahab. Others believe that Omri was her father and that Ahab was her brother who later took her and functioned as her own father. Some refer to her as Omri's granddaughter (see 2 Kings 8:18,26). The word "daughter" in 2 Kings 8:26 is from the Hebrew translation, "a daughter in the wide sense and in terms of relationships, a branch, or company."[32] Whether she was a daughter or a granddaughter, we see the full revelation of this translation representing even a "spiritual daughter" or one of the same "character and spirit" of Jezebel in operation. Using the term "branch" for the translation of "daughter" implies she was a branch or an offshoot from the "root" of Jezebel and Ahab.

The name, Athaliah, means "whom Jehovah has afflicted," meaning misery, pain, sickness or calamity.[33] Many times in Scripture, afflictions were caused by curses upon the generations due to the sins of the ancestors. Since Athaliah was a descendent of Jezebel, a curse of affliction came upon her. She, in turn, inflicted pain and calamity upon others. Her name is derived from a root word which implies "to handle violently." As you continue to read concerning Athaliah, you will recognize her violent acts of destruction as she destroyed the seeds of destiny in the generations. The spirit of Athaliah operates today with the same motive.

Athaliah was also the wife of King Jehoram of Judah and was Judah's only queen who ruled from 841-835 B.C. (see 2 Kings 11:2, 2 Chr 22, 23). Her husband is noted to have the same character and spirit of Ahab. Therefore, the daughter of Ahab and Jezebel married and came into agreement with a man with an "Ahab spirit!" Now, the planned strategies of the thief become even more intense. Let's examine the history of Athaliah more closely:

1. the daughter of Jezebel and Ahab had the same spirit of her parents
2. she married a king who had the same spirit as her father, Ahab
3. she inherited, by the bloodline, a hatred for true authority
4. she inherited, by the bloodline, idolatry
5. she inherited, by the bloodline of her mother, Jezebel, a determination to gain authority at any cost!

She, like her mother, Jezebel, worshipped the Canaanite god, Baal, and encouraged her husband to do the same.[34] Evidently, she had the ability to greatly influence and manipulate her husband, just as her mother controlled and influenced Ahab. Jezebel was the one who brought the false prophets and the idol worship of Baal into Israel. Now, her daughter had committed the identical act in Judah. "Judah" translates as "praise." Athaliah's intent was to destroy the praise of Jehovah and counterfeit the worship by praising the false god, Baal. Even today, the Jezebel spirit attacks the pure praise and worship of God by attempting to seduce worship leaders and members of worship teams into sin and apostasy.

With her motives set to gain more authority, she seized the throne as the "absolute power" in Judah upon her husband's and her son's deaths. Her son died from battle wounds (see v. 28) and she immediately began her "reign of terror" in Judah. She murdered all of her son's (Ahaziah's) male children because they were heirs to the throne (See 2 Kings 11:1).

The demonically-inspired plan to seize total control and power, regardless of the cost, was hatched by Athaliah and was twice as destructive as the reign of Jezebel. Similar to King Herod, who destroyed all of the male children as he sought to destroy Jesus, Athaliah destroyed anyone who threatened her throne of authority.

The only child in succession that was not murdered was Joash, her youngest grandson. Interestingly Athaliah's daughter, Jehosheba, took Joash and hid him from her mother for a total of six years. The queens own daughter fought for the rightful lineage to the throne and saved her nephew's life.

Athaliah ruled for six years and was finally slain before her seventh year of illegitimate authority in Judah. It was Jehoiada, the priest; who rose up and led a revolt against the queen of Judah. The crowning of the child, Joash, as the rightful heir brought about the death of Athaliah (see 2 Kings 11:5-20). The Scripture states that as the child was crowned, the people of Judah rejoiced, blew trumpets and declared "God save the King!" Athaliah cried out "Treason! Treason!" At that time the priest commanded for her to be slain. (Jezebel will ALWAYS falsely accuse others of acts that SHE is really committing!)

Looking more closely at the characteristics of Athaliah we notice these manifestations:

1. a murderous spirit
2. the thief in operation: she would steal, kill and destroy to have her way
3. jealousy
4. fear and intimidation
5. bitterness
6. rebellion
7. anger
8. pride
9. violent aggression
10. self-centeredness
11. false religion, Antichrist spirit
12. idolatry
13. manipulation
14. control
15. seducing spirit
16. falsely accuses
17. lies and deceit

Slaying the Spirit of Athaliah

Dear ones, it took a Jehu to destroy Jezebel. In order to slay Athaliah's seed, it will require the anointing of the priesthood! What does this mean to us today? Each of us is called as a "priest of the Lord" - chosen ones to serve Him. We are descendents of a royal lineage, called to show forth the praises of God as well as to rule and reign with godly authority.

> *But ye are a chosen generation, a royal priesthood, a holy nation, a peculiar people, that you should shew forth the praises of him who hath calleth you out of darkness into his marvelous light.*

1 Peter 2:9

Let's look more closely at a few characteristics of the priesthood:

1. the priesthood is consecrated
2. the priesthood is anointed
3. the priesthood are servants in the House of God
4. the priesthood is dedicated and committed
5. the priesthood is holy
6. the priesthood is clothed with righteous garments
7. the priesthood is to "utterly destroy all"

We can be assured of victory if we commit ourselves to purification and consecration. By utterly destroying all areas of defilement and committing to our destiny, we will overcome the seduction of the enemy. It is our season to take off the old garments, and exchange our clothing for the righteous garments of Christ Jesus.

Each time I travel to different churches, I recognize the demonic assignments against the next generation. The children of ministers are targeted by seducing spirits. Satan has planned strategies to destroy our seed and our children's seeds of destiny!

The Sure Mercies of David

Incline your ear, and come unto me; hear, and your soul shall live; and I will make an ever lasting covenant with you, even the sure mercies of David.

Is 55:3

God has promised us the same as He did King David. In the scriptures it speaks of the sure mercies of David. These "mercies" are the promises made to David and to his seed, or "lineage" of authority. God made a covenant promise with David that David's seed would rule upon the throne forever! No matter what happened, even if David's children backslid, God promised that David's children would have authority!

Saints, it is the same for us today. It may appear that the devil has snatched our children from us. It may seem as if we do not have the authority needed to protect our children. However, according to God's Word, our children have a seated position with Christ Jesus!

Jezebel and Athaliah tried to stop godly authority from rising up. The defeat of these two spirits will be caused by anointed Saints taking their rightful places in destiny and then destroying the demonic assignments.

Dear Ones, neither your destiny nor your seed's destiny will be aborted, because of God's covenant promise!

Chapter Fourteen

SHIFTING INTO DESTINY

I awoke to the radio music alarm. It was the morning of my sixteenth birthday. My heart was full of expectation and hope. I had been dropping LARGE hints to both parents that I desired a car for my birthday. I had been driving the family station wagon long enough; after all…I had an "image" to protect!

Was I getting my hearts desire today? Would I run from the house toward the garage and see my dream car fully materialized? I could visualize in my mind's eye that shiny red Stingray in full Technicolor….my palms began to itch waiting for the keys. (The Stingray was a car for "ancients")

I rolled over to turn off the alarm….and there they were! The keys to "SOMETHING!"

The entire situation struck wrong…I noticed the keys were not shiny and new. The key chain wasn't even new but rather had a worn appearance…like a hand-me-down set of keys. The shape of the keys reminded me of our 1943 tractor that I often rode. We lived on 7 acres and I was the family "mower" during the summer months. It took me a solid month to master shifting the gears of that old tractor. The transmission continually suffered as I would laboriously "grind" the gears and shift into higher speeds. I was always in a hurry to finish my mowing responsibilities. After all, I had more important things to do other than mowing a pasture. I had planned activities such as cheerleading practice, basketball camp and other pressing events.

"Come on you stupid tractor!" I would complain. "Can't you go any faster?" Well, what speed could you expect from an antique tractor?

I snatched up the keys and ran outside still holding onto hopes of pleasure. It is a miracle, I thought, as I continued to imagine my NEW car! In full speed, I burst through the back door and came to a screeching HALT as I took my first glimpse at my birthday present. There it sat, lifeless and still....and old. "What kind of car was it?" I thought to myself. "*WHAT* is it?" My mind raced backwards and I remembered seeing this type of car in my parent's family album. I recalled they had one similar to this when they first married....but that was over 25 years ago!

I stood breathless. What were these feelings I was experiencing? I finally had my own vehicle. I could now go anywhere in my own car....but could I be sure it would get me to where I wanted to go?

"Well, what do you think?" My dad proudly proclaimed his accomplishment for finding such a *rare jewel*. "I bought it yesterday. You have no idea how long I searched to find you just the right vehicle! What do you think of the color? It is a new paint job!" Obviously, it was a car that my dad loved. I think it was probably the same one he might have owned when he was a teenager!

I searched for the right words for an acceptable reply. Again, my thoughts raced as I dealt with my emotions and disappointments. The car was BLUE and not red. It was OLD rather than new. It was NOT what I had pictured nor desired. I began to force myself to smile and to focus on the fact that I now had my own car, regardless of what type of car it was. I determined to enjoy the vehicle because it still represented freedom and the "maturity" of having your own car. Talk about having to SHIFT!

That car became known as "the blue bomb" around my high school. The guys thought it was cool to own a 1951 Chevy. After all, it was a three speed, refurbished, with white walls...all formerly foreign words until I owned one. To me, it was clunky, blue and antique. I was into NEW and shiny and sophisticated! And besides, I did not do well with *shifting*. That old car would hang in neutral, as I would drive. That blue bomb caused me more frustration than I can put in words. But the one thing I definitely remember is that I detested the *shifting*!

Eventually I began to master the gears, and when it would get stuck in neutral I would determine to ride through it until I could get the transmission to shift properly. It took me a while to convince my dad that, though I only drove on "country roads," there may come a day that those country roads may not truly "take me home." My dream car came one year later. However, it was still a blue car and not red…but it was NEW!

Shifts Defined

A shift in the Spirit indicates that there is some type of *change* taking place. To shift gears in a vehicle indicates that one is changing direction or speed. A shift represents moving from one place to another, a changing of position or levels. When typing, we often use the "shift" key to change typing technique. No matter how we write the definition, a shift represents CHANGES.

Maybe you are like I was when attempting to *shift* gears in the Spirit. Sometimes, I got *stuck in neutral*. Often there was a grinding of gears as my rebellion toward God's changes occurred. All these areas of challenge would slow down my progress in God.

The Church is in a season of many supernatural shifts. God is shifting us from the old into the new. We are being challenged to let go of old religious mindsets and the slavery mentality of Egypt.

He is shifting us into destiny and as He does this He is purposefully speaking to us that in order to make this shift we must renew our minds.

As He shifts us out of Egypt we find ourselves in the Wilderness for a season. Then there comes the time when we must shift from the wilderness mentality into Canaan land…our Promised Land. The Promised Land is just what it proclaims, a land that is promised to us; a land full of fulfilled promises. In fact, it is our places of destiny. In order for us to pursue this promised place of fulfillment there must be a shift from doubt and unbelief into the place of great faith. It is a shift from death into resurrection. We are being shifted:

> …from the old wine to the new wine
> …from old wineskins into new wineskins
> …from religion into present truth
> …from old things into new things

The Crossing

As we move into this new place in God there are three phases that each of us must experience. First is a shift into deciding that we WANT to cross over into the Promised Land. Second is a shift into the actual place where we CROSSOVER the Jordan River. And the third phase is possessing our territory AFTER we cross over.

Shift ONE: The Decision

Making a decision is very hard for some of us. In fact, we will postpone decisions for fear of making the WRONG decision. But in this case, it is not simply a decision of crossing over into a new place, but rather deciding if we **want** to experience our "promise."

Most of us are aware of our promises from God. Whether it is a promise in the midst of a personal prophecy, a promise released through prophetic preaching and insight, or a promise that God shares with us during our intimate times with Him. Maybe you have been given a promise through a dream or a vision. At any rate, as the old adage goes....*a promise is a promise*! That is how God views His Word; if He promises, He is able to fulfill and complete that promise.

Webster's Dictionary defines a promise as a declaration that something either WILL or WILL NOT be done. I am reminded through this definition of God's promise that He will fulfill His part if we fulfill our part. Such as if we keep His words and commandments and remain obedient, we will eat the fat of the land. However, if we do not remain obedient and faithful to Him, we will not receive our promised inheritance! By this we understand that God's promises are often conditional.

Another definition for a decision is that it is a **determination** that arrives AFTER a consideration. In other words we cannot become determined for destiny (Promised Land) until we first make the decision that we want to cross over into our destiny. Wow! Just think about this. Many of us have been trying to focus in crossing over without first truly deciding that we **want** to cross over. We are attempting to move forward with determination without making the firm decision that we want to move forward.

The Lord began to speak to me about this one firm fact: WHEN I <u>DECIDE</u> TO TAKE MY PROMISE THEN THERE IS A SUPERNATURAL EMPOW-ERMENT THAT IS GIVEN THAT EQUIPS ME TO MOVE FORWARD!   It is at that precise moment that the shift takes firm root and comes forth into matur-ity.   Many of us have been trying to take our promised inheritance without fix-ing our faces like flint into destiny.   There can be no supernatural empowerment until decisions are made.   Once the decision is made, and we are firmly fixed on the promise, the Lord empowers us to move and shift into destiny!

Imagine yourself driving on a freeway.   You come to a "Y" on the interstate and you cannot decide which way to turn.   If you do not make a decision, you will end up going straight into a barricade or some other obstruction.   You will have an accident if you cannot decide.   You might waver back and forth, slow-ing down oncoming traffic, which could cause an accident.   You are in danger until you make a decision!   You cannot accelerate forward until you decide.   It is the same when making a spiritual decision to move forward.   There will be nei-ther empowerment nor acceleration unless you finally make the decision to move forward.   In fact, it will most likely be dangerous to try and remain in the middle of the road!

What will you decide?   You must decide to move forward from your place of confinement.   Most of us are confined to old patterns of behavior.   We have mindsets concerning areas of the Spirit.   We only know "church" the way we have been experiencing church.   We cling to familiar songs, hymns and ser-mons.   But, like Abraham, we must shift out of the old and proceed into new areas.   We are to leave what is comfortable and familiar to move into greater places of blessing.

Moses is Dead

The Book of Joshua begins with the Lord telling Joshua that Moses was dead.   Joshua knew that!   Why did God have to remind Joshua of that?   Was God trying to hurt Joshua with the remembrance of his mentor's death?   Was God being cruel?   No!   There was an entire move of God that was connected with Moses.   God was challenging Joshua to embrace an entirely new way of understanding Him.   God was about to do a new thing, and He needed Joshua to understand the new way.   God was about to move differently and lead His children differently. Spiritual leadership was shifting into a new dimension and Joshua needed to understand the shift from the old to the new.

Let's examine the first three verses of the book of Joshua to understand God's new direction.

> *Now after the death of Moses the servant of the LORD it came to pass, that the LORD spake unto Joshua the son of Nun, Moses' minister, saying, Moses my servant is dead; now therefore arise, go over this Jordan, thou, and all this people, unto the land which I do give to them, even to the children of Israel. Every place that the sole of your foot shall tread upon, that have I given unto you, as I said unto Moses.*

Joshua 1:1-3

Notice three instructions in the new direction:
1) RISE UP
2) GO OVER
3) YOUR FEET SHALL TREAD

No longer were they wandering through the wilderness. This was the season for Joshua to rise up and lead others to also rise up. We cannot move forward without first rising up. This means that we are to rise up from dead and desolate areas of our lives. We are no longer going to sit and wait but rather advance forward.

Next we are to go over the Jordan; this will involve another shift as we shift over into our new place. Yes, there may be some "grinding of the gears" as we decide to go forth. We may even get stuck in neutral for a while, but we must keep our eyes on the prize of the higher calling!

After crossing over into this new place, we are to begin to possess every place our feet tread upon. "To tread" means to trample and march upon; signifying a military march and possession. It means that we are to make our mark upon the land, to stake our claim and drive our stakes into the ground-laying claim to our inheritance! Just as a miner finds gold and stakes his claim, we are to cross over, knowing that the gold has been laid up for us, and then stake our claim to our ground!

By further studying the word *tread*, it implies making a great sound or a "sound of treading." In other words as we move forward as an army, we will make a great sound. Have you watched war movies and heard the sounds a marching army can produce? It is powerful! To the enemy it is a threatening, terrorizing and dreaded sound. The Lord was telling Joshua that as they took claim of their land that He would cause their footsteps to make such a great sound that it would cause the enemy to flee before them!

I am reminded of the three lepers who went into the camp of their enemy and the Lord magnified the sound of their feet. The enemy thought it was the sound of a marching army and began to flee. The three lepers took the spoils and then saved an entire city from starvation. The sound of treading is fierce and tormenting to our enemy!

We Need a Joshua

Most children of God do not realize this fact: in order to possess the promise, they need a Joshua and not a Moses leading them. God is causing a shift from a "save me" mentality to a "take me in" mentality. Though Moses was a very powerful leader, he was not the one that God used to possess the land. God had to raise up another leader, Joshua, who knew how to fight for the promise. Too many times Moses interceded for the people to save them from God's correction. Moses allowed the people to eventually wear him down to the place where he gave into the demands and whimpers of the people. Therefore, he himself could not cross over into his own promise.

We all need a Joshua. Though our flesh would like to hang onto a Moses, we need the new wine that the leadership of Joshua represents. What is this new wine? It is a new way, a new thing, a new direction.

Moses is similar to many pastors that function today. All too often they will allow their sheep to remain dependent upon them. They counsel by the hour and are there for the sheep at their demand. However, there must be a shift. Sheep do need intensive care at times. However, there must be a time when every sheep finds the will of God for his or her life and begins to mature. Moses interceded at times when perhaps he should have allowed God to discipline. Many pastors intercede whenever the Lord wants to discipline his sheep. We will never be able to cross over and fight for our land if pastors do not allow the children of God to fight for themselves. Many pastors are allowing co-dependent relationships in their flocks but God is raising up present day Joshuas who will lead His children into their inheritance.

This doesn't mean you have to leave your present church to receive the new wine. Many times our present leadership is trying to bring in a new move and we won't receive it! When we go through dry seasons we blame "MOSES" rather than asking God why we are so dry. So many times we will murmur and complain about our leaders, the programs, the way tithes and offerings are received…and all the while God is working on US! It is easier to blame Moses than to move forward with Joshua who represents CHANGE.

All too often we hold onto fears of authority, fears of failure, and our lack of faith. It is too easy to blame others for our personal lack of intimacy with God. We want to be like the Israelites. We want to be "saved" from our enemies rather than to RISE UP and possess our enemies. Moses interceded for the people; Joshua represented what I refer to as the DO IT YOURSELF ministry. In other words, pray yourself, anoint yourself, ask God yourself rather than calling someone else to do the work for you! So many Christians are too lazy to hear from God for themselves and too quick to blame others for their lack of discipline and breakthrough.

In this shifting, the Church is shifting from immaturity to maturity. It is time for the Church to grow up so we can "go up" to a new level of God's glory. All too often we have been like Moses in asking God to "show us Your glory" when God is trying to MOVE us so that we will see it!

As we mature, He is shifting us from the old cloud mentality into a faith mentality. In the wilderness, the camps moved as they followed the cloud by day and the fire by night. So many times I catch myself daydreaming of how easy that would be. As a pastor, I would not have to spend time in prayer seeking direction. I would simply get out of bed each morning, throw open the door and look for the cloud. I could easily tell the direction of the Lord with my natural eyes.

Unfortunately, in the shift from Moses to Joshua, the cloud and fire ceased. They could no longer move by what they saw in the natural, they began to move forward according to the WORD OF THE LORD! There was a new level of trust that the people had for their new leader. They didn't see clouds, fire, thunder or lightening any longer. They had to choose to hear the direction from their new leader, Joshua. There was a divine shift from seeing in the natural to *seeing by the Spirit.*

The directions were now coming from God to Joshua, then from Joshua to the congregation. The entire nation began to move into the promises based on hearing the Word of the Lord and "seeing" breakthroughs by the Spirit.

We are in the same place as Israel as they crossed over. We often cannot visualize the promise, but rather we must move forward with the eyes of faith. God has given each of us a promise, a word concerning our destiny, and in faith we must begin to tread through our promised land. As we tread, we will believe in faith that God is going before us and defeating our enemies.

The Second Phase: Crossing Over

A short season ago I was faced with a tremendous challenge. I had the opportunity to quit the ministry and begin selling real estate again. I was offered a financial increase with a very promising future. Since pastoring a church seemed overwhelming and demanding, I was faced with a decision that would affect my destiny. Though it was in my destiny to begin to travel more as a prophetess and be released from pastoring a local church, it was not the time. It was a temptation from the enemy; satan desired for me to commit spiritual fornication. Spiritual fornication is when we are offered something out of God's timing…yet we will eventually have it. The temptation was to leave my post before God released me.

I pressed into God, seeking an answer. My flesh wanted to go back to the old and familiar. I had been successful working in the world. I had been comfortable in my previous position, the previous salary and titles. I was not sure I could cross over into a destiny involving future ministry. It appeared too difficult. I felt as if I had nothing left to give God's children. I related often to Namoi in the book of Ruth. Naomi had lost her husband and her two sons. Suffering from desolation and lost hope, she encouraged her two daughters-in-law to go back home for she had NOTHING to give them! One daughter in law chose to go back home, but Ruth clung to her destiny link, which happened to be Naomi. As a result of Ruth clinging to Naomi, she came into great favor and later became fulfilled and married Boaz. In fact, Ruth later became one in the lineage of Christ.

Here I was, standing before my Jordan contemplating my future. Could I cross over this Jordan? Could I truly believe in His promises? Could I HOLD ONTO MY DESTINY LINK? (During tough times satan tempts us to let go of our destiny link, which are used by God to mature and empower us to move forward into our future. They are the teachers and mentors He uses to "process" us for ministry. Some destiny links are simply relationships that God uses to connect us with His future purpose and plan.) Was I willing to die more to my own desires, take up my cross to follow Him? As Naomi, I felt desolate and dead. I felt that I could go no further. However, as Ruth, I had to choose to cling to destiny!

When you feel dead and when you are the driest, God will tell you to "go a little further." In Matthew 26:39 Jesus was in the Garden of Gethsemane. He gathered His disciples together and then Jesus went a "little further" beyond them. There is a road that we come to that is called "a little further" and it comes at the "Y" in everyone's path. At that place along our journey we make decisions concerning our destiny. I have been at this crossroad several times since then, and each time I must become even more determined for destiny because I must take the road that reads, "a little further." DO NOT ALLOW DESTINY THIEVES TO STEAL YOUR FUTURE!

Those who desire ALL that God has for them will have to go a little further than others. Many stop short of full destiny. So many of us press through the wilderness and then come to a complete halt just short of crossing over the Jordan. Those who become determined will cross fully over. It is worth it, because at that time we will *shift* into the blessing. There will be seasons when you feel very alone. Do not allow the enemy to convince you that you are to separate yourself from like believers. You will feel naked and vulnerable and the devil will attempt to separate you from spiritual authority. Be on guard! Do not pull away! Rather, stay closely connected to your destiny link. Just as Ruth chose to remain close to Naomi, her destiny link, you will have to choose the same path. That pastor, that leader, that ministry may be the link to your destiny in God. Be cautious of moving too quickly and be sure you have heard from God before changing churches.

All too often God's children blame their dryness on others. We lose focus and vision and then blame others. Be careful during the crossing over period. You might get cold feet and decide to RETURN to Egypt. The leeks and garlic of the past seem inviting when you are staring into the challenges of moving forward.

Getting cold feet is part of the challenge of crossing over. After all, the priesthood stood in the Jordan for a long time waiting for all Israel to cross over. As a pastor, I feel that I have been in the Jordan, STANDING for years, and yes my feet get cold at times! Sometimes I want to run in the opposite directions from God's leading. My flesh screams, I get confused, I can't see, but I continue to choose destiny and remain with my destiny links.

You might be asking who my destiny links are. My spiritual father is Bishop Bill Hamon, the founder of Christian International. I know that the Lord placed me under his spiritual oversight so that I would be spiritually covered and would grow spiritually. Being linked with my Bishop links me with many others at Christian International. I need ALL of my destiny links to achieve God's full plan for my life. My husband and I both need destiny links. The ministers that we oversee also need destiny links. Also, members of every congregation need destiny links with their spiritual oversight. The plan of the enemy is always to disconnect us from our destiny links.

Think of a chain and its links. The links of a chain link together and form one continual chain of links. If we get disconnected, then that link on the chain is disconnected, and there is no longer oneness, a unity or a flow of connected links. When there is a spirit of disunity at work, there is a disconnecting. The Scripture says that unity brings life. The anointing is imparted from the headship down. When we become disconnected from authority, the oil of anointing ceases to flow down upon us. God is so very serious about unity. When we cross over the Jordan, we must crossover in oneness. If we can remain in unity then we will move forward with much greater power and authority.

A Song of degrees of David.

1) Behold, how good and how pleasant it is for brethren to dwell together in unity! 2) It is like the precious ointment upon the head, that ran down upon the beard, even Aaron's beard: that went down to the skirts of his garments; 3) As the dew of Hermon, and as the

dew that descended upon the mountains of Zion: for there the
LORD commanded the blessing, even life for evermore.

Psalm 133:1-3

As I have matured in God, I have moved from level to level in knowledge
and authority. Coming from a background of tremendous insecurity, I have had
to fight spirits of rejection many times. Also, the Amalekite spirit has continuously robbed me of many Aaron's and Hurs. At times, I was confronted with
false accusations, which opened old wounds of abandonment and rejection issues. I got cold feet so many times I wanted to invest in a stock of electric socks
and blankets to insure that would not happen again!

Do I Have to Get Cold Feet?

I have stood in the Jordan many times. Our leaders have stood in the Jordan over and over and over waiting for the entire congregation to decide to cross
over. If you remember, Joshua 3:8 states that the priests stood still in the Jordan
for a while. The waters flowing from Mt. Lebanon were icy cold and the priests
had to place their feet in ice water! Though the waters stood upon end and the
land eventually became dry to allow passage, there was a season of cold feet!
All of us, if we are following the Lord as priests, will be tempted to run as we
experience cold feet. But, if we can endure the process of crossing over, we will
be richly rewarded! Remember, any pain is a down payment for future gain.

The Third Phase: Possessing the Promise

Know for a fact, there are giants in your land! Just as Israel faced all the *ites*,
you will face your own. However, learn to fight your battles *from a place of*
victory. By this, I mean that we fight from the victory of our promise. God has
promised each of us a victory and as mighty soldiers we wage warfare with that
promise. Every promise becomes our sword of faith against the enemies that
stand in our land. First Timothy 1:18 states that we are to war a good warfare
over each of our promises (prophecies).

This charge I commit unto thee, son Timothy, according to the prophecies which went before on thee, that thou by them mightest war a good warfare;

1 Timothy 1:18

If you are ever tempted to go back to Egypt, or return to old ways of thinking or responding, remember the passage the Lord gave the children of Israel:

Only take heed to thyself, and keep thy soul diligently, lest thou forget the things which thine eyes have seen, and lest they depart from thy heart all the days of thy life: but teach them thy sons, and thy sons' sons;

Deuteronomy 4:9

We must always take heed and never forget what God has done for us. It is a truth and a testimony that we are to pass on from generation to generation. You will have to pray over your promises, proclaim your victories and wage warfare in the Spirit. At the time you experience the breakthrough you will have a powerful testimony of God's faithfulness.

Make a decision today that you will shift into your destiny. Become fixed and determined that you will cross over the Jordan that stands before you. Begin to exercise your faith and speak to every mountain and watch the Lord remove obstacles that are you before you. He is your Father and He desires to release your heart's desire. He will reward you as you diligently seek Him!

Becoming His Sharp Instruments:

*Behold, I will make thee a new **sharp threshing instrument** having teeth: thou **shalt thresh the mountains**, and beat them small, and shalt make the hills as chaff.*

Isaiah 41:15

Dear ones, it is time to take our mountain! We are to be His instruments of righteousness, his sharp threshing instruments...then we will experience our mountains moving!

In studying the translation of *sharp instrument* in this passage, it actually means making a decision and being determined. In other words our sharpness depends upon our determination. We cannot become a sharp instrument until we make a decision to serve God and be His instruments...only by being determined can we receive the supernatural empowerment to be sharp. Isn't this an awesome thought? God is simply waiting on us to rise up, like Caleb, and take what He has promised.

RISE   UP!!!

R espond
I n
S incere
E xpressions

U ntil
P urpose and destiny are accomplished

List below actions that you need to take to accomplish your destiny and purpose. What responses are needed?

Conclusion

CALEB'S INHERITANCE

Now therefore give me this mountain, whereof the LORD spake in that day; for thou heardest in that day how the Anakims were there, and that the cities were great and fenced: if so be the LORD will be with me, then I shall be able to drive them out, as the LORD said.

Joshua 14:12 (my emphasis)

Wouldn't it be awesome if each of God's children had the determination that Caleb possessed? Is it possible for us to discern the mountains that block our breakthroughs and confess that NOTHING is too difficult for the Lord? He can remove this obstacle? In faith, can we also proclaim *"now therefore give me this mountain?"*

Numbers 14:24 states that because Caleb had a different spirit he was able to take his land:

> *"...because all these men who have seen My glory and the signs which I did in Egypt and in the wilderness, and have put Me to the*

test now these ten times, and have not heeded My voice, "they cer-
tainly shall not see the land of which I swore to their fathers, nor
shall any of those who rejected Me see it. "But My servant Caleb,
*because he has a **different spirit** in him and has followed Me fully,*
I will bring into the land where he went, and his descendants shall
inherit it.

Numbers 14:22-24 (my emphasis)

By examining the previous passage it is clear that the Lord honored Caleb because he fully followed Him. Because of Caleb's faith in God's promises, he became even more empowered to take his possession, which was Hebron. The other Israelites, save Joshua, chose to believe the evil reports of the ten negative spies who saw their tribes as grasshoppers. The giants in their land appeared too big for the natural eyes. The spies chose to focus on the size of the enemy rather than the promises. They even brought back large grapes and the fruits of the land, but their mouths spilled negativity which overruled all of God's promises to them.

Israel chose to not heed God's voice. They chose defilement, the seduction of Egypt, along with old things and therefore were forbidden to cross over the Jordan into their inheritance. Notice in verse 24 it states that all of Israel had seen God's glory and the signs and wonders God performed on their behalf. Yet they continuously provoked God with their doubt and unbelief.

Because of the never ending murmuring and complaining, the land which was promised to them was closed off and they were not allowed to possess the promise. Only Caleb and Joshua crossed over into their place of possession along with an entirely new generation. The old generation, which included Moses, died in the wilderness. Joshua led the new army, an army that had a new belief system and a new wineskin, into the new land!

Taking Your Hebron

Caleb's inheritance was **Hebron**. The Hebrew translation for Hebron means "association, company and communion." In order to take the land of Hebron today it will require an army that is in covenant with each other - taking communion together as the Body of Christ in unity. Possessing new land requires unity, holiness and accountability. When the Body of Christ takes communion together there is a sense of unity and oneness. Communion is a representation of covenant relationships. Once the Body of Christ can truly become one with the Lord and His purposes, we can become one with each other. When the army is ONE then the battle is WON!

The word **Hebron** is derived from another root word and is translated as "spells and charms." This indicates witchcraft, sorcery and curses. As the Body of Christ moves into its rightful inheritance we will confront the occult powers of darkness. We will face wickedness, witches covens and territorial spirits head on. However, we need not fear because the Lord will go before us and slay our enemy. As we use the keys of the kingdom, binding the enemy and loosing God's perfect will, we will experience the full victory! The land of Hebron represents a promise for those who have the same spirit that Caleb evidenced. The same determination and empowerment can be ours, if we become *Determined for Destiny!*

The Grasshopper Mentality

"There we saw the giants (the descendants of Anak came from the giants); and we were like grasshoppers in our own sight, and so we were in their sight."

(Numbers 13:33)

Everyone has experienced fear. Children often fear the dark. Businessmen fear failure and financial loss. Pastors fear losing their congregations. Parents fear problems they may experience with their children. CEOs fear losing power or organizations. The Saints of God fear authority or spiritual abuse. EVERYONE experiences fear at some time in their lives.

The children of Israel experienced fear of the giants, who were descendants of Anak, a giant. Because they chose to focus on the giants rather than God's promise, they saw *themselves* as grasshoppers. Notice it does not say that the giants saw them as grasshoppers; the Israelites saw themselves as grasshoppers! The Israelites became intimidated due to the size of the giants.

So many times we focus on our limitations rather than choosing to believe what God says about us. God says we are not weak but strong. God says that we are chosen and blessed rather than insignificant. God says that we CAN when we confess we CANNOT!

The Israelites had murmured and complained for so long their hearts were consumed with negativity. They had sown into negative soil and could not begin to reap any positive fruit. If they had changed their "stinking thinking" then maybe a positive report could have surfaced. It is important for us to begin NOW believing the reports of the Lord! Let's begin to sow our words properly, believing that what God has said will come to pass.

Notice the characteristics of a grasshopper complex that are roadblocks to your possession:

Roadblocks to Possession

1. A doubting heart, negative speech
2. Unbelief
3. Distorted self-image
4. Inferiority
5. Lack of proper focus

God can do anything! He can heal your self image if you will commit to renewing your mind. By spending quality time in His Word and believing His promises your mind will be renewed. Faith comes by hearing and hearing God's Words. Spend time reviewing every personal prophecy you have received. Document the spiritual dreams and promises God has given. Begin to confess the Word of God over your life, your children, and your businesses. Remain focused on destiny and you will take your Hebron as Caleb was empowered to do!

You're never too old! It's never too late! Begin now...Take your Mountain!

How Do We Possess our Hebron?

1. Examine what you are speaking. Out of the abundance of the heart, your mouth will speak.
2. Wholly, completely, dedicatedly follow the Lord.

3. Have faith in God's promises.
4. Keep your eyes on God and not on your mountain.
5. Be strong and have courage.
6. Remember, once you decide on destiny, empowerment is released to fulfill destiny.

You Are Well Able To Take Your Land!

For I know the plans I have for you," says the LORD. "They are plans for good and not for disaster, to give you a future and a hope. [35]

Jeremiah 29:11

Saints, we can do what He says we can do! We are empowered by His Spirit to take our land. Hebron is ours, and just like Caleb, we can become empowered to take our promised mountain.

> # Go   For   It!
>
> ## DO NOT ALLOW THE DESTINY THIEVES
>
> ## TO STEAL YOUR DESTINY!

ADDITIONAL RESOURCES

From Sandie Freed

Title	Media	Price
Dream On (book) This insightful book offers us the tools we need to understand how God uses dreams to speak to us.	Book	$ 12.99
Dream On (cassette) This tape series will take you onsite of one of Pastor Sandie's *Dream On* seminars.	5 Cassette Series	$ 20.00
Dream On (workbook) This workbook goes hand in hand with both the book and the cassette tape series.	Workbook (8.5x11)	$ 10.00
Spiritual Discernment This 3 tape series will effectively teach you how to discern what God is saying to you. You will be stirred in a prophetic unction and activated in knowing the enemy's tactics.	3 Cassette Series	$ 15.00
The Process of Prophetic Fulfillment This 3 tape series will help you understand the process we all go through to fulfill our destiny.	2 Cassette Series	$ 15.00
From Glory to Glory Learn how to receive the fullness of God's manifest glory in your live and how to walk in His greater glory.	3 Cassette Series	$ 15.00
Overshadowed by His Glory	3 Cassette Series	$ 15.00
Resurrection Power	3 Cassette Series	$ 15.00
Times of Transition	2 Cassette Series	$ 10.00

To Order Contact:
Zion Ministries
P.O. Box 54874, Hurst, TX 76054
Phone: (817) 589-8811
Email: zionministries1@sbcglobal.net
Website: www.ZionMinistries.us

ADDITIONAL RESOURCES

(cont.)

From Mickey Freed

Title	Media	Price
Regaining Vision Pastor Mickey Freed explains the importance of FRESH vision in his new book "Regaining Vision". If you feel as if you have lost your hope and your spirit is perishing... this book is for you!	Book	$ 7.95
Opening Spiritual Gates This is a 3 tape series that deals with breaking open spiritual gates. Some Christians get to the threshold of their breakthrough and suddenly it seems that the forces of hell have come against them. We must remember, there will always be resistance at the threshold of your spiritual breakthrough.	3 Cassette Series	$ 15.00
Marketplace Ministry It is a must in this hour for the marketplace minister to take the gospel of Jesus outside the local church. Not only is the anointing to be used in the local church but also must be taken into the marketplace.	3 Cassette Series	$ 15.00
Exposing Witchcraft This is a 3 tape series that reveals the spirit of witchcraft. Although there are other spirits of witchcraft that are not discussed on this series, I believe rebellion, stubbornness, Jezebel spirits, and other witchcraft spirits are prevalent in and around the Body of Christ today causing havoc	3 Cassette Series	$ 15.00

To Order Contact:
Zion Ministries
P.O. Box 54874, Hurst, TX 76054
Phone: (817) 589-8811
Email: zionministries1@sbcglobal.net
Website: www.ZionMinistries.us

SPEAKING ENGAGEMENTS

To contact the author concerning
speaking engagements, contact:

Zion Ministries
P.O. Box 54874
Hurst, TX 76054
(817) 589-8811
Email: zionministries1@sbcglobal.net
Website: www.ZionMinistries.us

Sandie travels nationally and internationally speaking on dreams and visions as well as delivering the prophetic word to church congregations and ladies' conferences. She has a Masters Degree in Biblical Theology and has been a featured television and radio guest speaker on eating disorders, dreams and visions, and deliverance. Sandie has recently authored *Dream On* which not only discusses the importance of dreams and visions but also empowers every reader to interpret his own dreams.

Sandie also teaches seminars on How to Hear the Voice of God and challenges believers to release their faith to receive prophetic impartations and flow in the prophetic giftings. She is known for her powerful "down-to-earth" messages that release life transformation and encouragement.

For information on Zion Ministries seminars concerning The School of Prophets, Advanced Prophetic Training, Prophetic Intercession Training as well as recent teaching, books, tapes or itinerary, please call or contact the Zion Ministries website: www.zionministries.us.

RECOMMENDED READING

Davis, Dr. Jim. *Redefining the Role of Women in the Church.* Santa Rosa Beach, FL: Christian International Ministries, 1997.

Freed, Mickey. *Regaining Vision.* Bedford, TX: Zion Ministries, 2002.

Hamon, Dr. Bill. *Prophets and Personal Prophecy.* Shippensburg, PA: Destiny Image, 1987.

Hamon, Dr. Bill. *Prophets, Pitfalls and Principles.* Shippensburg, PA: Destiny Image, 1991.

Hamon, Dr. Bill. *The Day of the Saints.* Shippensburg, PA: Destiny Image, 2002.

Hamon, Jane. *The Cyrus Decree.* Santa Rosa Beach, FL: Christian International Ministries, 2001.

Pierce, Chuck D. and Rebecca Wagner Sytsema. *The Best is Yet Ahead.* Colorado Springs, CO: Wagner Publications, 2001.

Pierce, Chuck D. and Rebecca Wagner Sytsema, *The Future War of the Church.* Ventura, CA: Renew Books, 2001.

Yoder, Barbara, *The Breaker Anointing.* Colorado Springs, CO: Wagner Publications, 2001.

ENDNOTES

[1] *Webster's American Family Dictionary*, 1st ed., s.v. "destiny."

[2] James Strong, *The New Strong's Exhaustive Concordance of the Bible* (Nashville, TN: Thomas Nelson Publishers, 1984) ref. nos. 8615 and 6960.

[3] *Webster's American Family Dictionary*, 1st ed., s.v. "determined."

[4] Ibid., "thief."

[5] Ibid., "steal."

[6] Ibid., "secret."

[7] Ibid., "exposure."

[8] Ibid., "seduction."

[9] *Enhanced Strong's Lexicon,* (Oak Harbor, WA: Logos Research Systems, Inc.) 1995

[10] For more information concerning prophetic training and learning to discern the voice of God contact Zion Ministries at www.zionministries.us (817-589-8811) or Christian International Ministries in Santa Rosa Beach, Florida; www.christianinternational.org.

[11] Ibid.

[12] Dream On can be ordered by calling 817-589-8811 through Zion Ministries or by going to the website www.zionministries.us. Click on the product page, there are tapes available also. Also, there is a product page at the end of this book.

[13] 1 Samuel 1:17

[14] *Strong's Exhaustive Concordance*, ref. no. 1100.

[15] *Regaining Vision* can be ordered from the product page at the end of this book or by the website www.zionministries.us.

[16] *Strong's Exhaustive Concordance,* ref. 3290 and 6117

[17] Ibid., ref. no. 692.

[18] *Holy Bible, New Living Translation*, (Wheaton, IL: Tyndale House Publishers, Inc.) 1996.

[19] Ibid., ref. no 5221

[20] Strong's Exhaustive Concordance, ref. no. 2999.

[21] Ibid., ref. no. 4569.

[22] Ibid., ref. no. 3972.

[23] Ibid., ref. no 4613.

[24] Ibid., ref. no. 4074.

[25] Ibid., ref. no. 6003.

[26] Ibid., ref. no. 7497.

[27] *Webster's Dictionary*, "unclean."

[28] Ibid., re. no. 1294.

[29] Bill Hamon, *Prophets, Pitfalls, and Principles* (Shippensburg, PA: Destiny Image, 1991).

[30] Glenn Miller, *The Prophetic Fall of the Islamic Regime,* (Lake Mary FA: Creation House Press, 2004), p.69-70.

[31] *Webster's American Family Dictionary,* "generation."

[32] *Strong's Exhaustive Concordance,* ref. no. 1323.

[33] Dr. Judson Cornwall and Dr. Stelman Smith, *The Exhaustive Dictionary of Bible Names,* (Bridge- Logos Publishers, North Brunswick, NJ, 1984), "Athaliah."

[34] Walter A. Elwell, *Baker Encyclopedia of the Bible* (Baker Books, Grand Rapids, MI, 1997), Vol.2, p. 229.

[35] *Holy Bible, New Living Translation*, (Wheaton, IL: Tyndale House Publishers, Inc.) 1996.